For the Parent

The idea of this book came from my children, who had suggested that learning Hindi using traditional books and approaches was boring and learning the concepts through activity books was a much more entertaining way to learn a language. That got me thinking – if an activity book approach can be used to learn a language, why can't we use the same approach to teach the basics of Hinduism to our children growing up in the U.S.

This book is my humble attempt to teach Hinduism using an activity book approach. The concepts are introduced using activities such as matching exercises, crossword puzzles, matching activities and finding paths in a maze.

While all the nuances of a complex and rich religion like Hinduism can not be taught in a simple workbook like this, I hope your child will have fun as he or she explores the basics of Hinduism in this book.

Chanda Books
Email: chandabooks@optonline.net
Web: http://www.chandabooks.com

Copyright © 2008 by Dr. Dinesh C. Verma
Published by arrangement with Create Space Publishing

Table of Contents

Section I. Philosophy & Common Beliefs

Section II. Hindu Gods

Section III. Hindu Festivals

Section II. Hindu Calendar

For the Child

This book is an introduction to the Hinduism, one of the great religions of the world. It is followed by about a billion people in many countries all over the world.

Hinduism is old and has a tradition that goes back into the far reaches of history. Like any other ancient religion followed by a large number of people, it has many different branches and groups, each with their own practices and beliefs. However, there are many common concepts, principles and beliefs that are shared by all of the branches. The first section of this book explains those common concepts. The second section describes the Hindu gods and legends. The third section describes Hindu festivals and the last section some of the details in how time is kept in the legends.

Each concept of Hinduism is explained using puzzles of various types. If you complete the puzzles correctly, you earn stars that you can color in the bottom of the page. Once you have completed the book, count how many stars you have earned and check your level of understanding of Hinduism. A page which you can use to keep track of the stars you have earned is included at the end of this book.

The Philosophy
and
Common Beliefs
of Hinduism

Introduction

This section introduces the common beliefs that almost all branches of Hinduism share. All of the different branches of Hinduism share the common goal of making its practitioners happy and their main differences lies in the manner in which they think the state of happiness can be obtained.

If you want to go to a vacation in Florida, you can go there in many different ways. You can fly there, you can take a train, you can cruise on a ship to one of its coastal towns, or you can choose to drive. Each of these ways have the same end-result. However, they all have the same goal and many of the things you will do on the trips will be shared. They all will involve spending time with family, doing fun things on the way and eating out at nice places on the way.

In the same way, different branches of Hinduism take you to the ultimate happiness using different approaches, but they share many common ideas and concepts. These common ideas are what are covered in this section.

The Goal of Hinduism

Hinduism is a way of life. It is a collection of principles for thinking and acting which helps all of its practitioners achieve a goal. You can figure out the goal of Hinduism by solving the puzzle below.

To solve the puzzle, write out the name of each picture in the spaces provided to the left of it, using one letter per box. Then collect the numbered boxes together into the answer row to see the goal of Hinduism. After you have completed the activity, flip the book over to check your results.

Answer:

Color in the number of stars that you got from the activity on this page.

The Goal of Hinduism

Hidden in the puzzle on this page is a Sanskrit word which stands for happiness, the goal of Hinduism. Solve the puzzle to get that special word.

To solve the puzzle, write out the name of each picture in the spaces provided to the left of it, using one letter per box. Then collect the numbered boxes together into the answer row . After you have completed the activity, flip the book over to check your results.

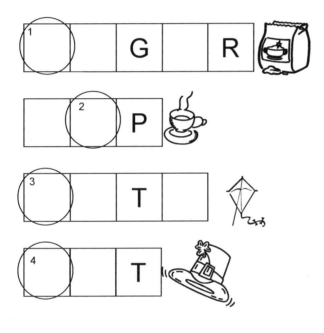

Answer:

1	2	3	4

Color in the number of stars that you got from the activity on this page.

What makes us Happy

There are four types of things that make us happy. Figure out the first type of things that make us happy by solving the puzzle below. Write down the name of the figure shown to its left and copy the numbered letters into the answer line. Note that the answer word is in Sanskrit. It is not an English word.

After you have filled in the letters for the answer, flip the book over to see how many stars you will get.

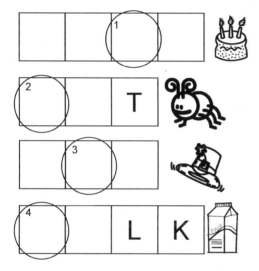

Answer:

1	2	3	4

Color in the number of stars that you got from the activity on this page.

What makes us Happy

The first category of things that make us happy are ones that give us physical pleasure. The generic term for all such things is *Kaam* (काम in Sanskrit).

From the list of things below, circle the ones that will fit into the category of physical pleasure or Kaam. Flip the book to see how many stars you get based on your answers.

A. Lots of money

B. Yummy Food & drinks

C. Love

D. Pretty Flowers

E. Have Fun

F. Power

G. Fame

H. Knowledge

If you selected B, C, D and E, give yourself 8 stars. Otherwise give yourself 2 stars for each of the choices of B, C, D and E that you selected. If you selected any of A, E, F, G or H, take away 2 stars for each such selection, but do not go below zero stars.

Explanation: Yummy food and drink, sweet smelling good looking flowers, having fun and finding love are all things that give us physical pleasure. Money and power by themselves do not give physical pleasure. Fame and knowledge are also things that are worthwhile, but don't give physical pleasure.

Color in the number of stars that you got from the activity on this page.

What makes us Happy

You can figure out the second type of things that makes us happy by filling in the names of the figures that are shown below. Solve the puzzle as before. The answer is a special word in Sanskrit – not an English word.

After you have filled in the letters for the answer, flip the book over to see how many stars you will get.

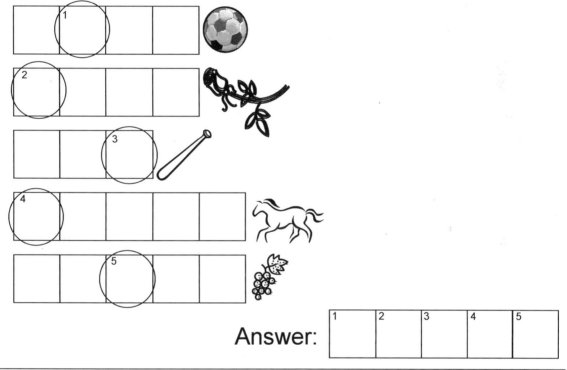

Answer:

1	2	3	4	5	

Color in the number of stars that you got from the activity on this page.

What makes us Happy

The second category of things that makes us happy are things that give us riches, power, influence and ability to make things happen. The generic term for all such things is *Artha* (अर्थ in Sanskrit).

The man shown on the left wants to reach the treasure chest on the right hand side. Find a path for him to reach the maze. You can only use adjacent stones to follow the path and only step on stones that show something that gives riches, power or influence to the person.

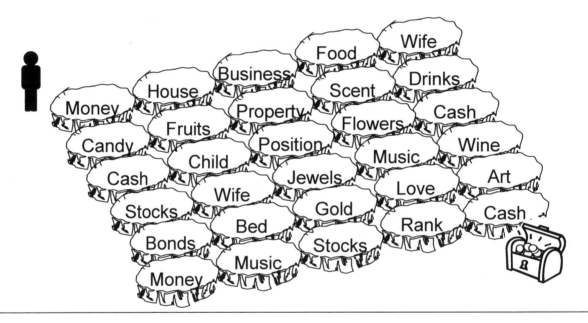

Explanation: The path listed above are the ones that show that a person has acquired riches and is able to use those riches. These include owning a house or property, getting a good job, collecting gold, jewels and other items and obtaining a high rank or position in society.

If you picked the path Money →House → Business → Property →Position → Jewels →Gold →Stocks →Rank —Cash , give yourself 8 stars. If you used any other nodes on the path, remove the corresponding number of stars from 8, but do not go below zero.

Color in the number of stars that you got from the activity on this page.

What makes us Happy

You can figure out the third type of things that makes us happy by filling in the names of the figures that are shown below. Copy the numbered letters into the answer line. It is a special word in Sanskrit – not an English word.

After you have filled in the letters for the answer, flip the book over to see how many stars you will get.

Answer:

1	2	3	4	5	6

Color in the number of stars that you got from the activity on this page.

13

What makes us Happy

Typically, after a person has obtained enough Artha, (wealth and riches), he or she wants to obtain things which falls in the category of *Dharma* (धर्म in Sanskrit). Dharma stands for the nature of a person or the duty that is expected of a person by other people in the society. The dharma of a person depends on his nature, upbringing and position in society. People want to do their dharma because they feel like helping others and want others to like them. In other words, doing their dharma makes people happy.

Match the positions listed on the left to the item in dharma listed on the right.

A. Soldier	1. Donates to charitable causes
B. Priest	2. Perform experiments to find nature of things
C. Scientist	3. Perform the rituals required at a wedding
D. Father	4. Nurse and love a newborn baby
E. Mother	5. Keep the school spic and span
F. Politician	6. Fight and kill the enemies in a battle
G. Janitor	7. Propose changes to the laws of a country
H. Rich man	8. Earn money, love and buy food for a child

The right answers are A-6, B-3, C-2, D-8, E-4, F-7, G-5, H-1. Color in as many stars below as you will gotten right in the list above.

Explanation: Dharma is determined by the occupation one picks in life, what one's position is and what one has a natural tendency to. You determine your dharma by understanding the expectations of others around you and fulfilling them. The goal of dharma is to make others around us satisfied. Being a social animal, every human being gets satisfaction by fulfilling the expectations of others and satisfying their inner calling. The matches above are the most reasonable ones.

Color in the number of stars that you got from the activity on this page.

What makes us Happy

There is a fourth and final thing that makes us happy. Figure out this thing by filling in the names of the figures that are shown below. Copy the numbered letters into the answer line to get the name of the ultimate thing we want.

After you have filled in the letters for the answer, flip the book over to see how many stars you will get.

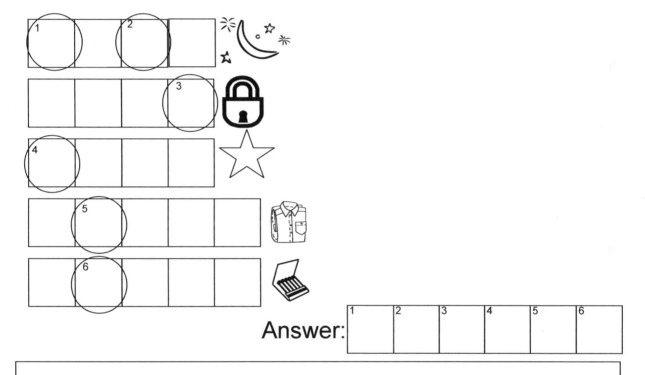

Answer:

1	2	3	4	5	6

Color in the number of stars that you got from the activity on this page.

What makes us Happy

Even after attaining Kaam, Artha and Dharma, many people yearn for something more. The happiness obtained by these three tend to be temporary. Hindu scholars have observed that some people are able to attain a state in which happiness is permanent. This state of permanent happiness is called *moksha* (मोक्ष in Sanskrit), roughly translated into eternal bliss.

Match the items listed below to the four categories in the center. Flip the book to see how many stars you get based on your answers.

1. Enjoy a funny movie

5. Build a temple (by a rich man)

2. Have a nice dinner

Kaam

6. Become a millionaire

Artha   Moksha

3. Get a well-paying job

Dharma

7. Marry off your daughter (by a father)

4. Feed a child (by a mother)

8. Get drunk on alcohol

The right answers are Kaam for 1, 2 and 8, Artha for 3,6 and Dharma for 4,5 and 7. Color in as many stars below as you will get then right.

Surprised that there is nothing that matches Moksha. Moksha is a state of mind, something that is entirely personal. Enjoying a movie and having a nice dinner are instant gratification and are kaam. Getting drunk on alcohol, drugs or an intoxicant is also physical pleasure, even though any smart person would avoid it because of their long term bad impact. Getting a job or becoming a millionaire is Artha, while a mother feeding her child or father marrying off her daughter is dharma since that is what is expected of them. Building a temple for other people is something a rich man does for others, so it is also dharma.

Color in the number of stars that you got from the activity on this page.

What makes us Happy

What is the difference between Kaam, Artha, Dharma and Moksha? The missing words in the diagram below shows one way to distinguish between these four things.

Use the key to decode the missing words and find out the difference between them. To decode the missing words, copy the letter corresponding to each symbol in the key to the box above that symbol. See how many stars you get by flipping the book over.

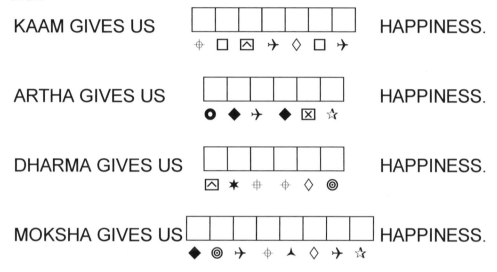

KAAM GIVES US [| | | | | |] HAPPINESS.

ARTHA GIVES US [| | | | |] HAPPINESS.

DHARMA GIVES US [| | | | |] HAPPINESS.

MOKSHA GIVES US [| | | | | | |] HAPPINESS.

Key															
Symbol	◇	⊕	☆	●	⊕	◎	⋏	□	★	⊠	⊡	✦	◆	⌘	■
Letter	A	C	E	F	I	L	M	N	O	R	S	T	U	V	Y

Color in the number of stars that you got from the activity on this page.

What makes us Happy

The four categories of kaam, artha, dharma, moksha are called purusharth, or things worthwhile getting in life. A person can obtain varying levels of all four. It is perfectly acceptable to achieve all of the four, or to just have one of the four. Generally a person can obtain increasing levels of happiness by shifting focus from kaam to artha, from artha to dharma and the maximum happiness is obtained by focusing on moksha.

We can use a four-bar chart to show how much emphasis a person places on each of the four items. The first bar shows relative emphasis on kaam, the second relative emphasis on artha, the third relative emphasis on dharma and the fourth the emphasis that person placed on moksha. A baby, e.g. would have all emphasis on kaam and will have a chart as shown in A below.

Match the other charts to the characters listed below. Flip the book to see how many stars you will get.

A. Baby   B.   C.   D.   E.

Characters: (1) The hare in the story of race between the Hare and Turtle (2) The turtle in the story of Hare and Turtle (3) King Midas in Greek legend (4) Adi Shankara - who re-established Hinduism in India in the eight century.

Color in the number of stars that you got from the activity on this page.

Obtaining Happiness

How does one attain the four objectives of Kaama, Artha, Dharma and Moksha?

Kaam is attained by a person via instinct. When you are hungry, your instinct will tell you what you can eat. Your body will tell you how to fulfill any craving you may have.

Artha and dharma are obtained by knowledge, skills and smartness one develops. You study medicine to become a doctor, study law to become a lawyer and learn trades/business skills to become a business man. Then you abide by your code of ethics, perform charitable causes and satisfy your social peers to attain dharma.

There is a secret Sanskrit verse hidden in code that tells how to attain artha and dharma. Decode it using the key. See how many stars you get from decoding it.

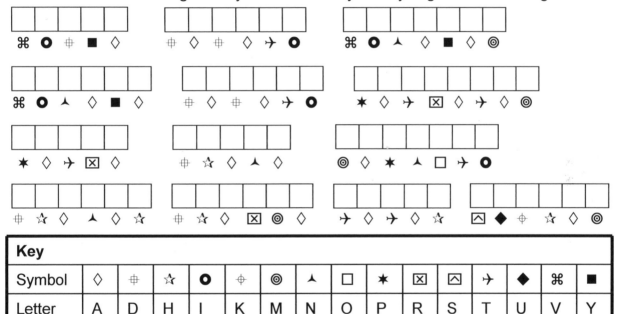

Key														
Symbol	◇	⊕	☆	●	⟡	◎	⋏	□	★	⊠	◲	✈	◆	⌘	■
Letter	A	D	H	I	K	M	N	O	P	R	S	T	U	V	Y

The verse is:Vidya dadati vinayam, vinaya dadati patratam, patra dhana mapnoti, dhanah dharma tatah sukham. It means: knowledge gives manners, manners give capability, capability leads to riches, riches lead to dharma and that leads to happiness. 8 stars for correct answer, 6 if you made a mistake.

Color in the number of stars that you got from the activity on this page.

Obtaining Happiness

One way to understand the concept of dharma is in terms of three debts. It is a great privilege to be born in this world as a human being. Hinduism states that each person is born with three debts on his/her head which needs to be repaid. Decode the three types of debts using the key below. Part of a person's dharma is to repay these debts.

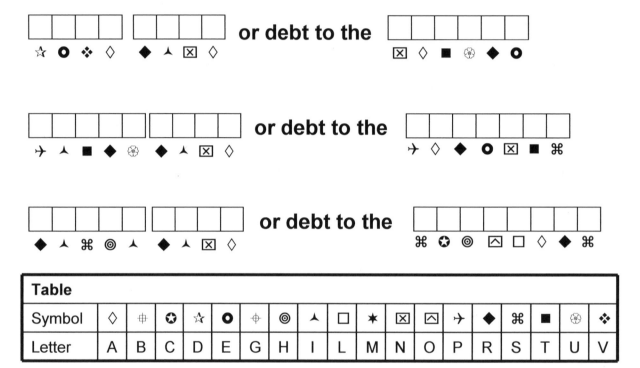

or debt to the

or debt to the

or debt to the

Table																	
Symbol	◇	⊞	✪	☆	●	⊕	◎	⅄	□	★	⊠	⊡	✈	◆	⌘	■	✿	❖
Letter	A	B	C	D	E	G	H	I	L	M	N	O	P	R	S	T	U	V

[The following text is printed upside-down]

Give yourself 8 stars if you get all six words right, otherwise 1 stars for each word you get right.

The three debts are DEVA-RINA or debt to the NATURE, PITRU-RINA or debt to the PARENTS and RISHI-RINA or debt to the SCHOLARS. We owe the debts to the universal spirit for bringing us in the worlds, to our parents for procreating us and to the scholars in our area who have passed their knowledge and know-how to us.

Color in the number of stars that you got from the activity on this page.

Obtaining Happiness

To repay each type of debt, we need to take some actions as part of our dharma. Some of the actions we can take to repay the debts are shown in the boxes below. Match them to the nature of debt we need to repay in the center.

Flip the book to see how many stars you get based on your answers.

| 5. Respect the divine forces on Earth |

| 1. Take Good Care of our Environment |

Debt to Nature

| 2. Pass on knowledge we have | | 6. Support those searching for knowledge |

Debt to Scholars

| 3. Seek to extend human knowledge | | 7. Earn money to maintain our children |

Debt to Parents

| 4. Get married and have children | | 8. Teach good habits to our children |

The right answers are Debt to nature for 1 and 5, debt to scholars for for 2,3 and 6 and debt to parents for 4,7 and 8. Color in as many stars below as you will getten right.

We repay our debt to nature by taking good care of it, preserving our environment and respecting the forces of nature. Many traditional Hindus include worshipping different gods representing the forces of nature as part of repaying the debt. Scholars include all people who have generated collective knowledge about our profession, e.g. the scholars who have given philosophy and theology, the scientists who have discovered laws of nature and if our job is that of a plumber, people who have accumulated knowledge in the art of plumbing. We pay our debts to our parents by marrying and having our own children and taking good care of them.

Color in the number of stars that you got from the activity on this page.

Obtaining Happiness

The following folk-tale illustrates the concept of repaying pitru-rina very well. Fill in the missing words in the right places from the table below to complete the story.

An eagle in the cliff was raising three (1)_____ chicks. He decided he should take them over to the opposite side of the deep valley where it was (2)_____. The chicks could not fly, so he clutched one chick gently in his claws and started for the other side.

In the middle of the flight, he asked, "Son, I am taking care of you right now. Will you take care of me when I grow (3)_____ and you are strong?" The chick replied, "How can you think of something so silly, father? No eagle never takes care of his father." "You (4)_____ child," screamed the eagle and dropped him in the valley to his death. Then he returned for the second chick.

He asked the same (5)_____ to the second chick in the middle of the trip. This chick, having seen the fate of its brother, replied, "Of course, Daddy. I will do everything to help you in the old age." The eagle screamed, "Liar! No bird has ever done so before, then how could you?" He (6)_____ the second chick too.

When the eagle asked the question to the third chick on the trip, it replied, "Father, I can't (7)_____ that I will take care of you, but I promise to take good care of any children that I have." The eagle (8)_____ at the answer of his son and took him safely across.

Table:
dropped, question, old, promise, safer, smiled, ungrateful, young.

Give yourself 1 star for each correct word that you got.

The correct mappings are (1) young (2) safer (3) old (4) ungrateful (5) question (6) dropped (7) promise (8) smiled.

Color in the number of stars that you got from the activity on this page.

☆ ☆ ☆ ☆ ☆ ☆ ☆ ☆

Obtaining Happiness

Obtaining Moksha, the ultimate thing anyone wants, is much harder than attaining the other types of purusharth.

How do we know that something like Moksha is attainable? It is because Hindu scholars have seen people obtain that state of ultimate happiness. They have also outlined the different ways by which this state of ultimate happiness can be obtained.

Each of these ways to obtain Moksha is called a marga (or path).

Find out which of the four people will be able to reach moksha in the center in the maze below.

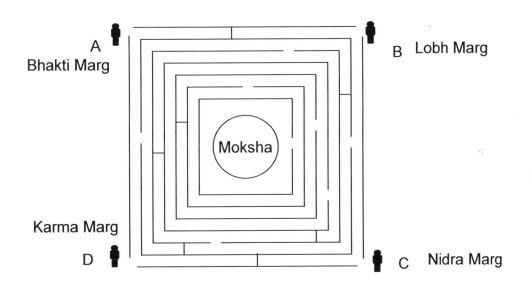

The people located at A and D can reach the goal of moksha. People located at B and C will not be able to reach moksha. 4 stars for each of A and D if you can find the path for them to reach moksha. If you know any Indian language, you will realize that Bhakti means devotion, Karma means action, lobh means greed and nidra means sleep. You could have used that as a clue.

Color in the number of stars that you got from the activity on this page.

Obtaining Happiness

Three different paths or margs that are commonly accepted as effective techniques to obtain moksha. The names of those three different paths are hidden in the letters below. To find out the names of the ways, cross out all occurrences of F,J,P,Q,S,U,X and Z from the sentences below

GFYANAXORJKNOWLEDGE,

AFCJTSIOPNOQRKARXMAZ,

BHAFKTIOJRDEVOTIXON

In the path of knowledge to attain moksha, a person would study scriptures, learn philosophy, logical reasoning, other branches of learning and use tools such as meditation and yogic exercises to train one's mind and body.

Give yourself 8 stars if you got all of the words. If you missed out a word, lose a star, but don't go below zero stars.

Did you get the following words - GYANA OR KNOWLEDGE, ACTION OR KARMA, BHAKTI OR DEVOTION?

Color in the number of stars that you got from the activity on this page.

Who we are

Before we get into the details of the different margs, let us look at who we really are. There is a special word that is used in Hinduism to represent who we truly are. Figure our that word by filling in the names of the figures that are shown below. Copy the numbered letters into the answer line to get the special word.

After you have filled in the letters for the answer, flip the book overto see how many stars you will get.

Answer:

1	2	3	4

Color in the number of stars that you got from the activity on this page.

Who We Are

The Atma (आत्मा in Sanskrit) is the spirit, force or power that makes you. Whenever you use the word I, it is the Atma that you are referring to. You are the Atma. The atma is the real you.

From the figures below, circle all the parts of your body that make up the Atma. Flip the book to see how many stars you get based on your answers.

A. Your Ear

B. Your Hand

C. Your Eye

D. Your Heart

E. Your Brain

F. Your Lungs

G. Your Tummy

H. None of the above

Explanation: The Atma is not a physical part of you. It is the spirit that drives your actions, the true part of you that remains unchanged as you grow from a child to an adult and will remain the same even if you change that part with a new one. Every atom making any part of you (your brain, your heart, your hands) will be replaced multiple times over in your life-time, but you, the Atma, will remain the same.

If you selected H, none of the above, give yourself 8 stars. Otherwise, subtract the number of choices you selected from 8 and give yourself that many stars.

Color in the number of stars that you got from the activity on this page.

☆ ☆ ☆ ☆ ☆ ☆ ☆ ☆

The Universe

There is a special word that is used in Hinduism to represent the power behind all of the Universe. Figure our that word by filling in the names of the figures that are shown below. Copy the numbered letters into the answer line to get the special word.

After you have filled in the letters for the answer, flip the book overto see how many stars you will get.

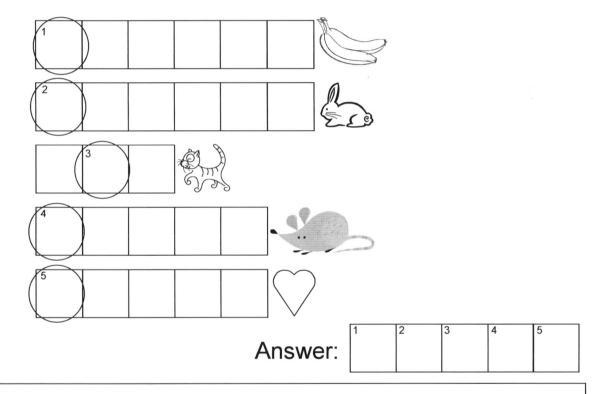

Answer:

1	2	3	4	5

The words are BANANA, RABBIT, CAT, MOUSE and HEART. The answer is BRAMH.

For each of the words that you got correct, give yourself one star. If you got the answer right as well, give yourself 3 more stars. If you got all the words and the answer right, you will get 8 stars.

Color in the number of stars that you got from the activity on this page.

The Universe

The Bramh (ब्रम्ह in Sanskrit) is the spirit, force or power that drives the entire Universe. Like the Atma, the Bramh is an abstract entity. It is the force that drives all things in the Universe, physical as well as non-physical.

From the figures below, circle the components of the world that are controlled by the Bramh. Flip the book to see how many stars you get based on your answers.

A. The Oceans

B. The Planets

C. Peace

D. The Sun

E. The Earth

F. Weather

G. War

H. All of the above

Explanation: The Bramh is the universal spirit that drives everything in the world. It is the power behind the principles of physics, chemistry and biology. It is manifests itself in things that are physical, e.g. the oceans, the planets, the sun and the moon, as well as things that are abstract, e.g. peace, war, happiness and suffering that exists in the world.

If you selected H, all of the above, give yourself 8 stars. Otherwise, subtract the number of choices you did not select from 8 and give yourself that many stars.

Color in the number of stars that you got from the activity on this page.

Path of Knowledge

People who follow the path of knowledge read the scriptures, discuss philosophy and try to increase their knowledge about the Atma and Bramh. The code message below tells how the path of knowledge can lead to moksha.

Decode the message provided by this code. Flip the book over to see if you will getten the right message. Check how many stars you get.

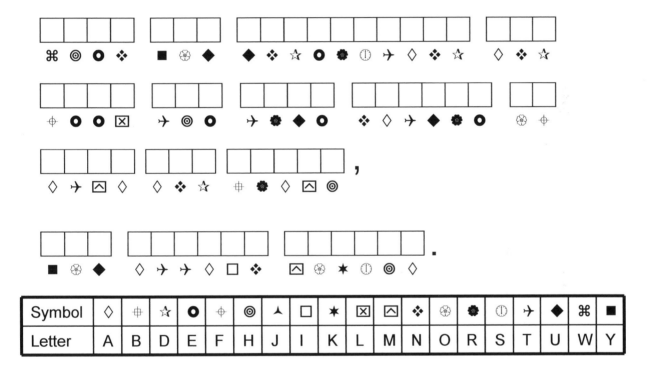

Symbol	◇	⊕	☆	●	⊕	◎	⏶	□	★	⊠	◹	❖	⊛	❀	◔	✈	◆	⌘	■
Letter	A	B	D	E	F	H	J	I	K	L	M	N	O	R	S	T	U	W	Y

Color in the number of stars that you got from the activity on this page.

Path of Knowledge

Those who followed the path of knowledge in the past have made several observations which are accepted by most Hindus. Solve this cross-word puzzle to determine one of these observations.

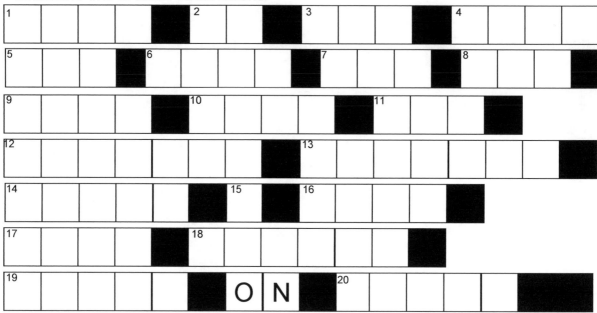

Hints:
1. The spirit of a person
2. Present tense of was
3. A negative statement
4. Coming into this world
5. Conjunction
6. Add an es after do
7. Something that says no
8. Leaving this world
9. Fair in giving justice
10. Not love but _____
11. Smallest number
12. not remains the same
13. What you wear
14. Opposite of Before
15. First letter of alphabet
16. Cleaning with water
17. Same as in first hint
18. to rotate or alter
19. Plural of a body
20 The act of dying.

Color in the number of stars that you got from the activity on this page.

Path of Knowledge

A person following the path of knowledge reads many different types of books and scriptures to understand the nature of Atma and Bramh. If you cross out the letters B, C, L, M and X from the list of words below, you will get the names of some of those books.

BTHCEFLOUMRVEZDAXS,

CXTHEUMPZANISCHADS,

BCANXDTLHEPMURANAS

LMXCBZBZXLMBLMZCB.

Color in the number of stars that you got from the activity on this page.

Path of Knowledge

The four Vedas are the fountainhead of knowledge in Hindu tradition. They contain a description of Hinduism's rituals, philosophy and a wealth of advice, anecdotes, prayers and cures for various types of illnesses.

Decode the names of the four vedas by writing the letters in the boxes corresponding to their symbols using the key below.

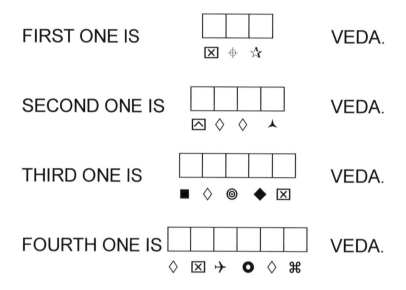

FIRST ONE IS ⬜⬜⬜ VEDA.

SECOND ONE IS ⬜⬜⬜⬜ VEDA.

THIRD ONE IS ⬜⬜⬜⬜⬜ VEDA.

FOURTH ONE IS ⬜⬜⬜⬜⬜⬜ VEDA.

Key															
Symbol	◇	⊕	☆	●	⊕	◎	⅄	□	★	☒	◹	✈	◆	⌘	■
Letter	A	C	G	H	I	J	M	N	O	R	S	T	U	V	Y

Give yourself 2 stars for each word you decoded correctly above.

The four decoded words are: RIG, SAAM, YAJUR and ARTHAV. The RigVeda is the oldest one. The Rigveda, Saamveda and Yajurveda focus on the different rituals, prayers and philosophy, while the Atharvaveda has a significant more focus on medicine and cures.

Color in the number of stars that you got from the activity on this page.

Path of Action

In the path of action to attain moksha, a person performs his or her duty, but without any desires of a resulting benefit. As an example, a student studies because it is his duty, he is performing duty without any benefit in mind. If a student studies because his daddy has promised him a toy if he gets a good grade, that is with a benefit to be desired.

Circle the actions being performed in the list below without any desire. Flip the book to see how many stars you get based on your answers.

1. A man establishes a charity so he will become famous.

2. A person donates his blood at Red Cross Event.

3. A student prays in the temple to get good grades.

4. A mother feeds her child.

5. A thief steals a car.

6. A politician passes new laws to benefit the people of the country.

7. A politician passes new laws so he will establish a legacy

8. A father works to earn the maximum for his family.

The right answers are 2, 4, 6 and 8. Color in two stars for each right answer you got.

Explanation: Each of the persons is performing his dharma. However, in 1, the man has the specific desire of getting fame. In step 2, the donation is without any desired benefit – assuming the donor is not getting money or showing off to his friends. The prayer in 3 is for a specific desire. Step 4, a mother is doing her duty simply. Step 5, the thief is stealing the car for his benefit – stealing is not the dharma of any person. A politician is expected to pass new laws to benefit his country, so 6 is action without desire, but 7 is not. In 8, the father is simply doing his duty assuming all the money is for his family.

Color in the number of stars that you got from the activity on this page.

Path of Action

Doing action without any desires is very hard. What happens if one performs actions with a desire of some type. Hindu scholars who have followed the path of knowledge, tell us that all action carries with it the results of the desire or intent with which the action is performed. If the person does actions with a good intent, good things accrue to the person as a result. On the other hand, if a person does actions with a bad intent, eventually he or she ends up paying for action with the bad intent. That is the concept of *karma*. The cycle of getting rewards or punishment is broken if we do actions without any desires. Escaping from this cycle is a way to attain moksha.

The Circle diagram below shows some good actions that are filled in. Fill in the opposite circle in the diagram with the same action which is performed with the opposite intent. Flip the book to see how many stars you get based on your answers.

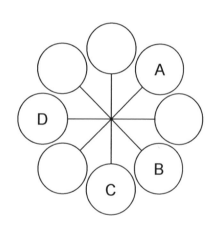

A. A doctor cuts a man to save his life with surgery.

B. A man makes a temple so people have a place to pray.

C. A mother scolds her child so he learns good manners.

D. A boy fights to save his friends from bullies.

1. A man makes a temple so he will be famous.

2. A mother scolds her child because she had a tough day.

3. A boy fights to scare all the other kids in neighborhood.

4. A robber cuts a man with a knife to threaten him.

The right answers are A-4, B-1, C-2 and D-3. Claim two stars for each right answer you got.

Explanation: Although the action performed in each of the case is the same, the intents are very different and that makes the same action have different impact on the person doing that action. Actions performed with good intent bring good things in the future and actions performed with bad intent bring bad things in the future. That is the law of karma – Good karma (actions) follows you and brings good things to you and bad karma brings bad things in your future. Some scholars say that karma will follow an atma past death into the next body an atma is born in.

Color in the number of stars that you got from the activity on this page.

Path of Devotion

In the path of devotion, one attains the ultimate happiness by selecting an object of affection. The object of affection could be a great person, anything you admire, someone you have seen other people admire, or an abstract principle. Then the follower in the path of devotion devotes his life to the object of affection. Many Hindus choose a manifestation of the Bramh, e.g. Rama or Krishna, as the object of their devotion.

Devotion helps a person to do actions in life without desire. If you are devoted to something else and looking after their interests and desires, you will end up performing actions without desiring anything for your own benefit.

Select the four objects among the eight listed from A-H that you think will be the best objects for your devotion. Flip the book to see how many stars you get based on your answers.

A. A giant whale swimming in the ocean

B. A famous saint from the past

C. A hero who did great things for society

D. A great scholar from the past

E. Your parents

F. A snake from the garden

G. A stone image

H. A tree or a forest of trees

There are no right answers. The four items you picked are worthy of devotion are completely up to your choice, depending on what you consider worthy to be devoted to.

Personally, I would have picked B, C, D and E. However, any choice you have picked are right. The Hindu tradition says that every person is free to pick whatever they want to worship or select as their object of affection.

Color in the number of stars that you got from the activity on this page.

Path of Devotion

Prayers play a big role in the path of devotion. A prayer may consist of rituals, praise or song offered to the object of devotion.

When you pray, the object of the prayer (be it a stone, a image or an abstract entity) serves to channel and focus your mind and emotions. This focus brings peace and happiness to you and gives you strength, will and determination. As long as you have faith and devotion in the object being worshipped, you will get the good benefits of prayer. Those benefits emanate from you and the object of the prayer is just a means to channel your strengths.

People ask for many things in prayers and the strength of will they get in the prayer allows them to achieve miraculous things.

The puzzle below makes a statement about prayers made to an object of devotion. Decode it? Check how many stars you get.

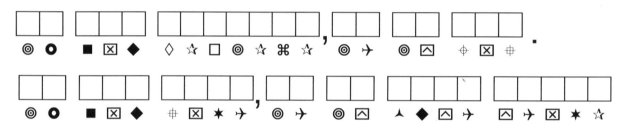

Key														
Symbol	◇	⊕	☆	●	⟡	◎	▲	□	★	⊠	◿	✈	◆	⌘	■
Letter	B	D	E	F	G	I	J	L	N	O	S	T	U	V	Y

The phrase is: If you believe, it is God. If you don't, it is just stone. The idol is a God only because you have faith in it and faith helps you become stronger. If you have no faith, it is a mere stone without any powers. In Hindi, the original saying is – maano to bhagwaan, na maano to patthar.

Give yourself 8 stars if you get it all right. Take two stars away if you made a mistake.

Color in the number of stars that you got from the activity on this page.

Path of Devotion

There are many ways that people following the path of devotion express their love and devotion. The object of devotion is these ways is the Bramh, or a representation of the Bramh. One of the means for expressing devotion is shown in the puzzle below. Name the objects in the figures and then assemble the letters in the numbered boxes to find the name of that method to express devotion. After you have filled in the letters for the answer, flip the book over to see how many stars you will get.

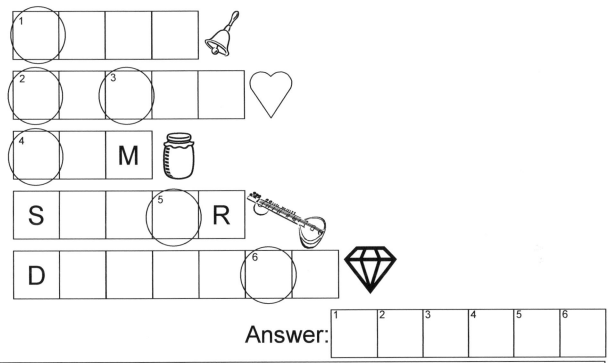

Answer:

1	2	3	4	5	6

The words are BELL, HEART, JAM, SITAR and DIAMOND. The answer is BHAJAN. A bhajan is a poem which is sung or recited in praise of the object of devotion, e.g. one could recite a prayer to Krishna, or Ram.

For each of the words that you got correct, give yourself one star. If you got the answer right as well, give yourself 3 more stars. If you got all the words and the answer right, you will get 8 stars.

Color in the number of stars that you got from the activity on this page.

Path of Devotion

In addition to the Bhajans, people following the path of devotion use other techniques to show their devotion to the manifestation of Bramh they have selected as the object of their devotion.

Find some of the things people on this path do by decoding the missing words using the key. Flip the book to see how many stars you get from decoding it.

They sing about the object of devotion in group with music.
This is called doing the

◎	●	⊠	✈	◇	□

They worship the object of devotion individually or in group.
This is called doing the

⊠	★	★	⊕	◇

They tell stories and legends about the object of devotion to each other.
This is called doing the

◎	◇	✈	☆	◇

Key														
Symbol	◇	⊕	☆	●	⊕	◎	⊼	□	★	⊠	⊠	✈	◆	⌘	■
Letter	A	C	H	I	J	K	M	N	O	P	R	T	U	V	Y

Give yourself 2 stars for each word you decoded correctly above and 2 bonus stars if you get all three.

The three decoded words are: KIRTAN, POOJA and KATHA. Together with Bhajan, these four activities are things people undertake on the path of devotion. All of these four activities can be performed while living a normal life, i.e. performing your dharma and living in the society.

Color in the number of stars that you got from the activity on this page.

☆ ☆ ☆ ☆ ☆ ☆ ☆

Paths Compared

Each of the paths has their own strengths and weaknesses. Depending on the nature of a person, some path may be more suitable than others.

Match the people marked below with specific nature to the three paths that are most suitable for them.

Flip the book to see how many stars you get based on your answers.

A. A studious person who likes to read books

B. Someone who likes reason and logic

C. Someone who is very intelligent

1.   Path of Knowledge

D. Someone who can control his or her emotions

E. Someone who likes to be active and dynamic

2.   Path of Action

F. Someone who is very emotional

G. Someone who finds studying boring

3.   Path of Devotion

H. Someone who likes music and songs

The path of knowledge is most suitable for someone who likes to study, logic and reason about things. It appeals to people who are highly intelligent and like intellectual challenges. The people with nature of A, B and C will find path of knowledge more suitable. The path of action is for people who want to be active, perform a lot of actions, but are able to take those actions without desires or emotions. People of nature D and E will tend to prefer the path of action. The path of devotion is the easiest among all three paths. It can be followed by anyone with average intellect and average nature. Someone who is emotional, does not enjoy serious philosophical discussions, but would love to sing and dance in prayers would like the path of devotion. So, F, G and H are more likely to follow the path of devotion.

Although any person can follow any path he chooses, the selections above would seem to fit their natural tendencies. Claim eight stars if you matched the nature to the right path as described above.

Color in the number of stars that you got from the activity on this page.

The Teacher/Guru

There are a lot of details in each of the path that are left for an individual to decide. Which books of philosophy to read in the path of knowledge, what set of actions to take in path of action, how does one train oneself to do action without desire, what is the best object of devotion in the path of devotion, or what is the best way to show and express one's devotion, etc. In Hindu tradition, each person is responsible for making these decisions on his/her own.

A teacher or Guru is a person who helps others make such decisions. The guru also helps people decide details about what their proper dharma is. A guru is a more experienced or learned person who can help a person tremendously. However, the guru is just a guide. The final decision is always the individual's.

Be careful in the choice of the guru. A bad guru can lead one astray.

Identify what type of teachers would be good or bad to pick for yourself in list below. Flip the book to see how many stars you get based on your answers.

A.   A teacher who asks you for your money to liberate you from bad kaam/artha.
B.   A teacher who says you should trust his judgment and not your own.
C.   A teacher who wants you to follow what is written in a book without thinking.
D.   A teacher who likes to drink and take drugs.
E.   A teacher who helps out other in the community.
F.   A teacher who wants you to make your own decisions.
G.   A teacher who is knowledgeable about other religions and beliefs.
H.   A teacher who tells you to renounce the whole world.

A good teacher would always encourage his/her followers to use their own brain, thinking and reasoning power. Anyone who says that you should not use your own thinking, but follow blindly any other person or the contents of a book is asking you to give up your own reasoning power and is not a good teacher. Someone who is taking drugs or alcohol which interfere with your thinking is likely not a good teacher. Someone who is asking you for money could be a crook trying to take you for a ride. A good teacher should be past the stage of wanting kaam and artha.
Accordingly, A, B, C and D are attributes of a bad teacher and E, F, G are attributes of a good teacher. H could be either good or bad depending on situation. Give yourself 1 star for H and then one star for those in A-G you identified correctly.

Color in the number of stars that you got from the activity on this page.

Summary of Common Beliefs

So far, we have described all the concepts that most of Hindus generally believe in. This page lists a summary of those common beliefs.

The common beliefs of Hinduism are:

1. That there is a atma in every person.

2. That there is a force called Brahm driving the Universe.

3. That atma does not get born or die with the physical body.

4. That it is natural of a person to seek pleasures (kaam), power (artha) and do one's duty (dharma) which give him or her happiness.

5. That a greater happiness than either kaam, artha and dharma exists, which is the state of moksha.

6. That each person is individually responsible for his or her own decisions/actions.

7. That the type of actions one takes impact the person in the future.

8. That there are many ways of obtaining moksha, including path of knowledge, the path of action and the path of devotion.

9. That the choice of a right teacher can help people tremendously in their search for happiness and moksha.

In an ancient religion like Hinduism, there are many differences of opinions as well. The next few pages list some of the ways in which different groups of Hindus differ.

Branches of Hinduism

There are many different branches of Hinduism. They all differ in their definition of what moksha is and the right way to get to moksha.

Fill in the names of the pictures shown below and arrange the numbered letters together to get the name of a branch of Hinduism. Guess what this branch believes in over and beyond the set of common beliefs?

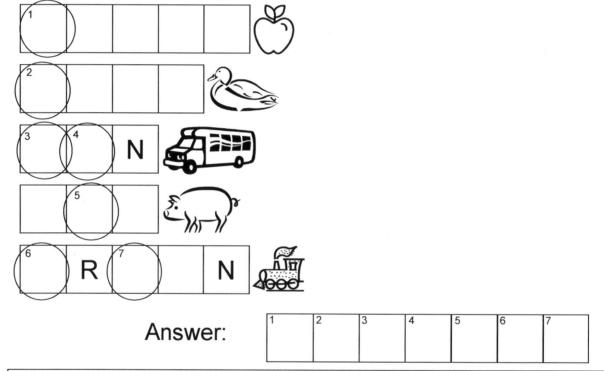

Answer:

1	2	3	4	5	6	7

Color in the number of stars that you got from the activity on this page.

Branches of Hinduism

The Advaita branch believes that Atma and Bramh are one and the same entity. Moksha is obtained when an individual realizes and feels the unity of these two. The Atma and Bramha were never really separated and people live under the illusion (called maya) that the two are separate.

There are four coded Sanskrit phrases below which are called the great insights of Advaita branch of Hinduism. Decode it using the key. See how many stars you get from decoding them.

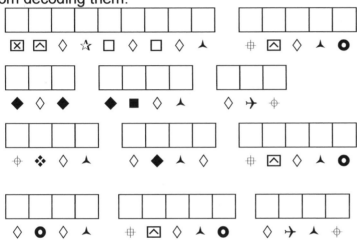

Key															
Symbol	◇	⊞	☆	●	⊕	◎	⋏	□	★	⊠	◁	✦	◆	⌘	■	❖
Letter	A	B	G	H	I	K	M	N	O	P	R	S	T	U	V	Y

Color in the number of stars that you got from the activity on this page.

Branches of Hinduism

We looked at the Advaita branch of Hinduism and what they believe in. There is another branch that believes that Atma and Bramh are two very distinct entities. Moksha is a state of happiness which the Atma obtains by coming closer to the Bramh.

Fill in the names of the pictures shown below and arrange the words together to get the name of this branch of Hinduism.

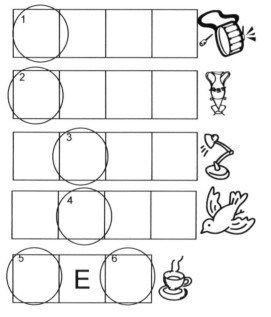

Answer:

1	2	3	4	5	6

Color in the number of stars that you got from the activity on this page.

44

Branches of Hinduism

Different branches of Hinduism have their own concept of what Bramh is. To find some common concepts of Bramh, remove all instances of B, C, X, Y, Z, G, L and M from the letters below. Then copy the remaining letters to get the different types of Bramh.

BCXSYAZCGLUMXNACB

XYNBCILRMXGLMUNAC

LSMZYAXACKBALABRY

CNXIYZRALNMKACALR

Did you get Saguna, Nirguna, Saakaar and Nirankaar? Give yourself two stars for each correct answer.

Some Hindu branches believe that Bramh has attributes (guna in Sanskrit), others believe it is without any attributes (nirguna). The former believe in saguna Bramh, the latter in nirguna Bramh. Those who believe is saguna Bramha also disagree whether or not Bramh takes a physical shape. Some believe Bramh takes physical shape (it is Saakaar) and others believe it never has a physical shape (it is nirankaar).

Color in the number of stars that you got from the activity on this page.

Branches of Hinduism

A large number of Hindus believe in Saakaar Bramh, i.e. they believe that Bramh takes a physical form and appears as a god to help humans and others. There are different branches of Hinduism which maintain that one particular form of Bramh is the best one to follow to obtain moksha.

Fill in the names of the pictures shown below and arrange the words together to get the name of a form that many people believe the Bramh takes.

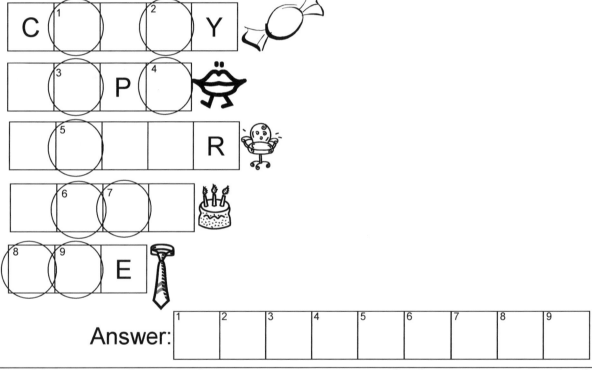

Answer:

1	2	3	4	5	6	7	8	9

For each of the words that you got correct, give yourself one star. If you got the answer right as well, give yourself 3 more stars. If you got all the words and the answer right, you will get 8 stars.

The words are CANDY, LIPS, CHAIR, CAKE and TIE. The answer is ADI SHAKTI. It is considered the ultimate mother goddess by many branches of Hinduism.

Color in the number of stars that you got from the activity on this page.

Branches of Hinduism

The Adi-Shakti is the first form of Saakaar Bramh. It literally means – the original force. Hindus who believe following the path of devotion to Adi-Shakti or its different forms are known as Shakts. Adi-Shakti is the female form of God.

Adi-Shakti gives rise to three male gods.
Decode the names of the three gods using the key below.

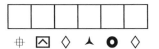

Key															
Symbol	◇	⊕	☆	●	⊕	◎	⋏	□	★	⊠	◩	✈	◆	⌘	■	❖
Letter	A	B	G	H	I	K	M	N	O	P	R	S	T	U	V	Y

Color in the number of stars that you got from the activity on this page.

Branches of Hinduism

A group of Hindus believes that the best path to obtain moksha (as well as Artha and Dharm) is by following the path of devotion to Vishnu.

Fill in the names of the pictures shown below and arrange the words together to get the name by which people following this branch of Hinduism are known.

Answer:

1	2	3	4	5	6	7	8

The words are VAN, BIRD, SHIP, NECKLACE and WAVE. The answer is VAISHNAV.

For each of the words that you got correct, give yourself one star. If you got the answer right as well, give yourself 3 more stars. If you got all the words and the answer right, you will get 8 stars.

Color in the number of stars that you got from the activity on this page.

Branches of Hinduism

The essence of following the Vaishnav branch has been described in a nice poem by the Gujarati poet Narsi Mehta. Fill in the words to the translation of his poem?

Only those deserve to be called (1)_____,
who feel the pain and (2)_____ of other people.
If they do something to help people in trouble
they do not become proud of their (3)_____.
They respect everyone in this world
and do not (4)_____ about anyone behind their back.
Their talk and action is (5)_____ and straight-forward
and they make their mothers proud of them.
They treat everyone in an equal fashion and are free of greed,
and are respectful of the opposite gender.
They never lie and don't steal from others
and are not enamored of worldly possessions.
Their devotion is (6)_____ in the name of Ram,
and they keep their body and thoughts holy like a place of pilgrimage.
They are free of (7)_____, cunning and trickery,
and abstain from anger, lust and mindless physical pleasures.
Narsi says that men like these bring others closer to god,
and meeting them inspires (8)_____ to follow the right path.

Table:
 charity, generations, gossip, greed, honest, sorrow, steadfast, Vaishnav

Claim a star for each right mapping of a word in the table to one of the blank spaces in the poem.

The right words are: 1. Vaishnav, 2. sorrow, 3. charity, 4. gossip, 5. honest, 6. steadfast, 7. greed, 8. generations. The original lyrics start as "Vaishnav jan to tene kahiye je, peer parai jaane re." It is a beautiful song to hear in the original Gujrati.

Color in the number of stars that you got from the activity on this page.

49

Branches of Hinduism

A group of Hindus believes that the best path to obtain moksha is by following the path of devotion to Shiva. Shiva is a god who gets pleased very easily and grants wishes to devotees quickly.

Fill in the names of the pictures shown below and arrange the words together to get the name by which people following this branch of Hinduism are known.

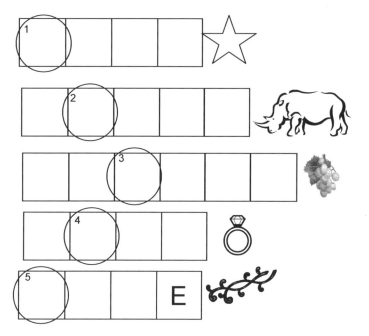

E

Answer:

1	2	3	4	5

The words are STAR, RHINO, GRAPES, RING and VINE. The answer is SHAIV.

For each of the words that you got correct, give yourself one star. If you got the answer right as well, give yourself 3 more stars. If you got all the words and the answer right, you will get 8 stars.

Color in the number of stars that you got from the activity on this page.

Saakaar Bramh
or
The Hindu Gods

Introduction

A large section of Hindus believe in Saakaar Bramh, i.e. they believe that Bramh takes a physical form which can be seen and felt. This form of Bramh is called dev, devata, bhagwan or god. Worshipping any of these gods and following the path of devotion leads to moksha.

Hindu scholars say that all of these forms of god are one and the same entity, so it does not matter which form we choose to worship. However, different branches choose to worship one form preferentially.

Of the three male forms of Saakaar Bramh, the two gods worshipped commonly are Shiva and Vishnu. Bramha is not worshipped commonly.

There are many other forms of gods that are worshipped, including Ganesh, Laxmi, Ram, Krishna and many others.

Even when different branches of Hinduism worship different gods, they usually accept that the worship of the other gods is a viable path to attain moksha as well. Generally, each branch has its own set of reasons explaining why the form they have chosen to worship is the better one.

In this section of the book, we learn about some of these various forms of gods, as well as some of the stories associated with them.

Adi-Shakti

The Adi-shakti gives rise to the three gods Bramha, Vishnu and Shiva. It also gives rise to the goddesses that consort with them, as well as other goddesses.

The name of the goddess of knowledge, also the wife of Bramha is shown below. Fill in the names of the pictures shown below and arrange the numbered letters together to get the name of this goddess. Flip the book to check how many stars you get.

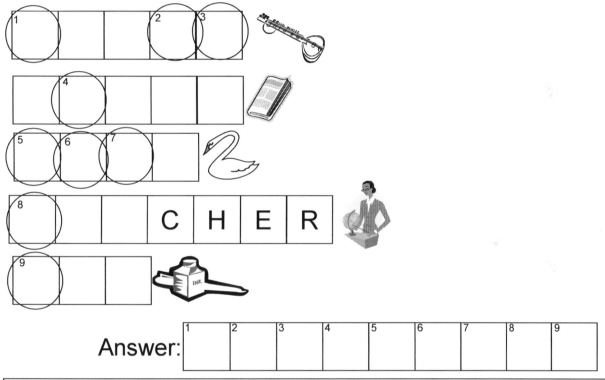

Answer:

1	2	3	4	5	6	7	8	9

Color in the number of stars that you got from the activity on this page.

Adi-Shakti

Another form of the Adi-Shakti is the goddess of wealth. She is also the wife of Vishnu. Figure out her name by filling in the names of the pictures shown below. Then arrange the numbered letters together to get the name of this goddess.

Flip the book over to see how many stars you will get.

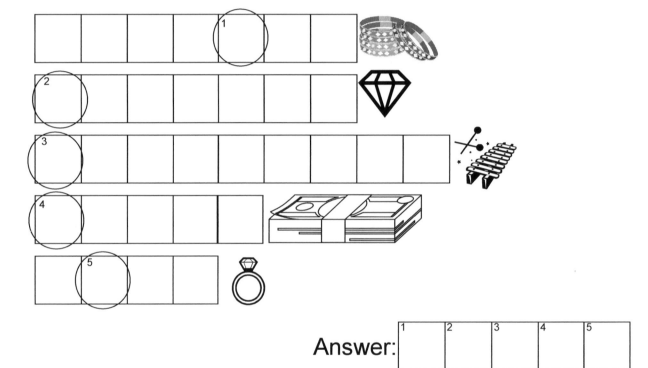

Answer:

1	2	3	4	5

Color in the number of stars that you got from the activity on this page.

Adi-Shakti

Another form of the Adi-Shakti is the wife of Shiva. Figure out her name by filling in the names of the pictures shown below. Then arrange the words together to get her name.

Flip the book over to see how many stars you will get.

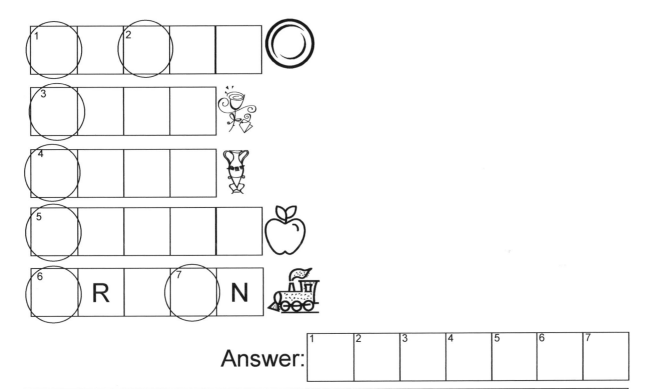

Answer:

1	2	3	4	5	6	7

Color in the number of stars that you got from the activity on this page.

55

Adi-Shakti

Adi-Shakti, the original female form of Brahm, gives rise to all other forms including many goddesses. Each goddess exhibits some attribute of the Adi-Shakti.
Match the names of the goddesses shown in the left column with the description in the right column.

Flip the book over to see how many stars you will get.

1. Durga

2. Kali

3. Sarawswati

4. Laxmi

5. Gayatri

6. Parvati

7. Radha

8. Sita

A. The goddess as destruction

B. The goddess as wealth

C. The goddess as destroyer of evil

D. The goddess as knowledge

E. The goddess as a model wife

F. The goddess as embodiment of pure love

G. The goddess as source of all chants

H. The goddess as an ascetic

Give yourself 1 star for each correct mapping.

The right mapping is 1.C, 2. A, 3. D, 4. B, 5. G, 6. H, 7.F, 8.E. The stories in the following pages provide more details.

Color in the number of stars that you got from the activity on this page.

Bramha

Although Bramha is the creator, he is rarely worshipped by Hindus. There is only one temple in the whole world devoted to Bramha at Pushkar in Rajasthan. Fill in the blanks in the following legend which explains why Bramha is not worshipped widely. The missing words are shown in the table at the bottom.

One day, Bramha and Vishnu started arguing as to who was more capable. (1)_____ happened to come by as the other two were arguing and proposed a (2)_____ to settle the dispute. He would create a large pillar and the other two would try to find its end in opposite directions. Whoever found the end of the pillar and returned first would be declared more capable.

Bramha and Vishnu flew off on their mounts to find opposite ends of the (3)_____. Vishnu went on flying till his mount (4)_____ got tired. He gave up and returned back to Shiva acknowledging his inability to find the end. Bramha was searching on the other side and could not find the end either. However, he saw a ketaki flower in the middle of the pillar and thought of a trick. He asked the (5)_____ flower to act as a witness and returned with it to Shiva, claiming he had found the end.

But Shiva had created the pillar to be endless. Bramha's lie was caught. For lying, (6)_____ was declared not worthy of worship. Ketaki, which was false (7)_____, is also never used in any rituals. (8)_____ won the challenge.

Table:
 Vishnu, Ketaki, Garuda, pillar, Shiva, witness, Bramha, challenge

Give yourself 1 stars for each correct word that you got.

The correct mappings are (1) Shiva (2) challenge (3) pillar (4) Garuda (5) ketaki (6) Bramha (7) witness (8) Vishnu.

Color in the number of stars that you got from the activity on this page.

Bramha

At the beginning of each cycle of creation, Bramha creates many different types of species. These include all types of animals, birds and people.

According to legend, three species of living beings had the most amount of consciousness. Use the key below to determine who those three species of living beings were.

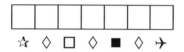

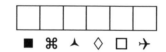

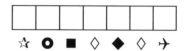

Key																
Symbol	◇	⊕	☆	●	⊕	◎	▲	□	★	⊠	◹	✈	◆	⌘	■	❖
Letter	A	B	D	E	H	K	M	N	O	P	R	S	T	U	V	Y

The three species with the most level of consciousness are DANAVAS, HUMANS and DEVATAS.

Humans were the weakest among these three groups. Danavas, also known as daityas or asuras, were powerful and strong species. They also tended to be cruel and tended to treat humans badly with only a few exceptions. Devatas, also known as suras or devas will be equivalent to gods in English. They usually tended to treat humans in a more friendly manner. The danavas and devatas had frequent conflicts among themselves to assert dominance over each other.

Give yourself 8 stars if you get all three, otherwise give yourself 3 stars for each word you get right.

Color in the number of stars that you got from the activity on this page.

Bramha

The following story about devatas, danavas and humans teaches a moral about how to behave. Fill in the missing words in the right places from the table below.

After creation, the danavas, devatas and humans settled the different worlds. The danavas were dominant force in the Universe. The devatas had a nice happy life full of riches and pleasures. And the humans worked the earth and lived off its treasures. However, none of them were truly happy. All three races sent a delegation to (1)_____ to find out how they could become happier.

To each delegation, Bramha replied that their way to happiness begins with the letter d. The humans interpreted it as daan or sharing. They had plenty of riches from the earth and they started (2)_____ it with other humans and other species that lived on Earth. The danavas interpreted it as dayaa or (3)_____. They started treating those under their control with kindness. The devatas interpreted the d as daman or (4)_____. They started to control their indulgence in pleasures. All three species found they were much happier after following their interpretation of d.

If in life you have power, follow Bramha's advice and show kindness to those in your (5)_____. If you have riches, (6)_____ a bit with those who are not as lucky. And if your life is full of (7)_____ and fun, try to exercise self-restraint. These help you become (8)_____ in life.

Table:
Bramha, control, happier, kindness, pleasure, share, sharing, self-restraint.

Give yourself 1 stars for each correct word that you got.

The correct mappings are (1) Bramha (2) sharing (3) kindness (4) self-restraint (5) control (6) share (7) pleasure (8) happier.

Color in the number of stars that you got from the activity on this page.

☆ ☆ ☆ ☆ ☆ ☆ ☆ ☆

59

Vishnu

Vishnu has many names by which he is called. The table below lists 16 of these names. Find these names in the matrix below. Each name either goes up-down, left-right or diagonally across the matrix using adjacent boxes.

For each word that you get, award yourself with half a star. Round up to the nearest whole star.

Keshav	Vishvakarma	Shyam
Suresh	Achyuta	Janardan
Srinivas	Vishwatma	Ram
Narayan	Siddharth	Sripati
Hari	Madhav	Loknath

M	A	D	H	A	V	N	K	P	L	V	J
S	Q	K	E	S	H	A	V	A	O	I	A
U	S	V	L	R	S	R	T	C	K	S	N
R	A	M	P	I	R	A	T	H	N	H	A
E	U	L	M	P	N	Y	D	Y	A	V	R
S	S	H	Y	A	M	A	K	U	T	A	D
H	A	R	I	T	R	N	E	T	H	K	A
S	R	I	N	I	V	A	S	A	V	A	N
V	I	S	H	W	A	T	M	A	G	R	S
S	I	D	D	H	A	R	T	H	T	M	N
A	M	R	I	T	Y	A	U	V	N	A	R

Color in the number of stars that you got from the activity on this page.

Vishnu

Vishnu has many names. There is a prayer which recites a thousand names of Vishnu. Some of these names have meanings. Match the eight names of Vishnu in the left column with the meaning of that name in the right column.
Use the hint table below to make your job easy.

1. keshav	A. Master of the entire world
2. svayambhoo	B. The atma of the universe
3. dhaataa	C. The creator of the universe
4. sarvaadi	D. The dispenser of fruits of action
5. vishvakarmaa	E. The origin of everything
6. sarveshvar	F. He who is born from himself
7. vishvaatma	G. One with beautiful hair
8. lokanaath	H. The controller or everybody

Hint: Break each name into its sub-words. The you can figure out the meaning using the following meanings of the sub-words.

kesh = hair   svayam = self   bhoo = born from
sarva = everything   aadi = beginning   vishva = universe
karmaa = creator   eshvar = controller   lok = world
Naath = master

The mapping is 1.G, 2. F, 3. E, 4. D, 5. C, 6. H, 7.B, 8.A. Give yourself 1 star for each correct mapping.

Color in the number of stars that you got from the activity on this page.

Vishnu

Vishnu is responsible for the preservation of the Universe. In order to do so, Vishnu has to continuously ensure that order is maintained in the Universe. Use the hints below to figure out a sentence about Vishnu.

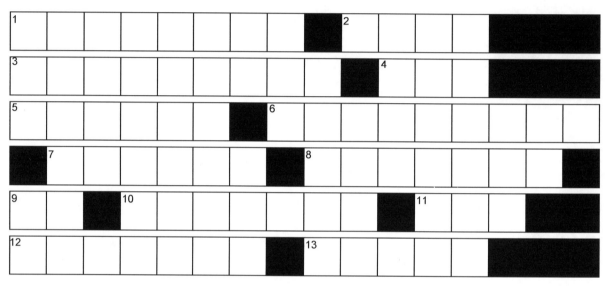

Hints:

1. At every or any time something happens
3. Growing in size or volume
5. The third purusharth
7. The title of this page
9. Sounds like the number two
11. Most commonly used word in English
13. When you sort a list, you put it in _____.

2. Bad, sinister or not good
4. Conjunction
6. Reducing in size or volume
8. Coming or reaching
10. To reestablish
12. Occurring in Nature

The sentence is: Whenever Evil increases and dharma decreases, Vishnu arrives to restore the natural order.

Give yourself 8 stars if you get all 13 words, otherwise give yourself 1 star for each 2 words you get right.

Color in the number of stars that you got from the activity on this page.

Vishnu

Each arrival of Vishnu in the Universe is for a purpose. There are ten major arrivals of Vishnu that happen in each chaturyuga (see the section on time-keeping). Each arrival is called an avatar or incarnation. Match the ten avatars of Vishnu in the left column with his actions on the right column.

Flip the book over to see how many stars you will get.

1. Meen (Fish)   A. Help extract treasures of the seas

2. Kurm (Tortoise)   B. Trick a danav king was very generous

3. Varaah (Boar)   C. Bring the land out from the seas

4. Narshimh (Man Lion)   D. Save the ancestor of current human race

5. Vaaman   E. Be the role model for behavior

6. Parsuram   F. Teach the path of action to humanity

7. Ram   G. Save earth from cruel warrior kings

8. Krishna   H. Remove cruel and inhumane rituals

9. Buddha   I. Will come in the future

10. Kalki   J. Save a devotee from his father

Give yourself 1 star for each correct mapping up to 6 correct ones. Then half a star for each additional correct mapping.

The right mapping is 1.D, 2. A, 3. C, 4. J, 5. B, 6. G, 7.E, 8.F, 9.H, 10.I. The stories in the following pages provide more details.

Color in the number of stars that you got from the activity on this page.

Vishnu

The following story tells a story about the time when Vishnu took the form of a fish. Fill in the missing words in the right places from the table below.

It was the end of the previous chaturyuga cycle. Manu was out in the river and scooped up some water in his hands. There was a small fish he had gathered by accident. He was about to drop it back when the fish pleaded for him not to drop it back. It was afraid that the big fish in the river will eat it up. (1)_____ took it back and kept it in a small pot.

Soon the fish had grown big enough to fill the (2)_____ and it pleaded to Manu to transfer it to a bigger pot. The fish was growing rapidly and it soon outgrew every pot that Manu had. Manu transferred it to a pond, but the fish soon grew bigger than the pond. Manu transferred the (3)_____ to a river and when it grew too big for the river to the sea.

Finally, Manu could not contain his curiosity. He asked the fish who it really was to grow such (4)_____ large in such a small amount of time. The fish revealed that it was (5)_____ and warned Manu about a flood that would destroy all of humanity. When the flood came, Manu was saved by the fish. The fish left Manu at the very top of a (6)_____.

When the waters receded, Manu met Shradhha, another survivor. Manu and (7)_____ were ancestors of all humans at the start of this cycle of (8)_____.

> Table:
> chaturyuga, Manu, pond, Vishnu, mountain, pot, fish, Shradhha, miraculously

The correct mappings are (1) Manu (2) pot (3) fish (4) miraculously (5) Vishnu (6) mountain (7) Shradhha (8) chaturyuga. If you want to know what a chaturyuga is, do the activities in the section of the book on Hindu time-keeping.
Give yourself 1 stars for each correct word that you got.

Color in the number of stars that you got from the activity on this page.

Vishnu

The devatas and danavas figured out that a lot of treasures were hidden in the sea. They decided to churn the sea using the serpent Vasuki as a rope and the mountain Mandar as the churn. But the mountain was sinking in the sea, so Vishnu took the form of a tortoise to keep the mountain afloat and help the churning.

The churning produced many treasures. Decode the name of a few of those treasures using the key below.

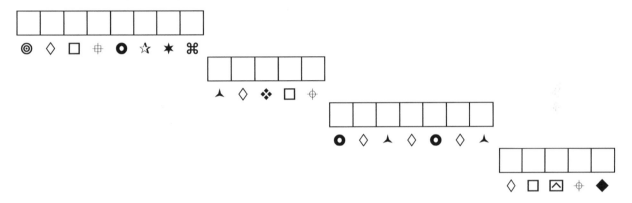

Key																
Symbol	◇	⊞	☆	●	⊕	◎	▲	□	★	⊠	⬑	✈	◆	⌘	■	❖
Letter	A	D	E	H	I	K	L	M	N	P	R	S	T	U	V	X

Give yourself 8 stars if you get all four, otherwise 2 stars for each word you get right.

The four treasures listed above are Kamdhenu, Laxmi, Halahal and Amrit. Kamdhenu is the divine cow that produces anything one wants. Laxmi is the goddess of wealth. Halahal was a very strong poison which could have destroyed the world. Shiva ingested it and kept it in this throat which turned blue from the poison. So Shiva is called neelakanth (neel = blue, kanth = throat). Amrit is a drink which makes anyone drinking it immortal. The devas tricked the danavas out of the Amrit. The churning of the sea produced many other treasures as well.

Color in the number of stars that you got from the activity on this page.

Vishnu

The following passage tells the story of Vishnu as the Boar and the half-man half-lion. Fill in the missing words in the right places from the table below.

A danav hid all of the land under the oceans. Vishnu took the form of a boar, brought the land to the surface on his (1)_____ and killed the danav. The danav's brother, now the new king of danavs, started to hate Vishnu. He went to war against Vishnu and the devatas. In the fight between the danavs and devatas, the (2)_____ queen of danavs was captured by the devatas. She had a son, Prahlad who was raised by the devatas. He became pious and a devotee of Vishnu. When the war was over, (3)_____ and his mother returned to their father.

Prahlad's father, the danav king, had a boon which said that he could not be killed by a devata, a man or any type of (4)_____. He could not be killed at day or at night. He could not be killed on earth or in the sky. And he hated Vishnu with all his heart. When he found out his son Prahlad was a (5)_____ devotee of (6)_____ , he was very angry.

He ordered Prahlad to stop worshipping Vishnu. When Prahlad would not give up, he tried all ways to kill his own son. When Vishnu protected Prahlad at all stages, the demon father decided to tie him up to a pillar and kill his son himself. Vishnu came out of the (7)_____ as a half-man and a half-lion, put the demon on his lap so he was neither on earth nor in sky and killed him in the (8)_____ when it was neither day nor night. Thus, he saved Prahlad.

Table:
pregnant, tusks, animal, Prahlad, Vishnu, pious, evening, pillar

Give yourself 1 star for each correct word that you got.

The correct mappings are (1) tusks (2) pregnant (3) Prahlad (4) animal (5) pious (6) Vishnu (7) pillar (8) evening.

Color in the number of stars that you got from the activity on this page.

☆☆☆☆☆☆☆☆

Vishnu

The following passage tells the story of Vishnu as the midget. Fill in the missing words in the right places from the table below.

The grandson of Prahlad, Mahabali was a great warrior. Under his leadership, the (1)_____ conquered all of the Universe. The devatas were unhappy at their defeat and they appealed to Vishnu for help. They pointed out that while Mahabali himself was a noble king, the danavs as a group were cruel to humans and other living things and should not be allowed to remain in charge of the Universe. Vishnu agreed and devised a trick to help the (2)_____ regain control. He took birth as a small midget or vaaman.

Mahabali was a (3)_____ king who ruled justly and helped all those who where in need. The (4)_____ went to Mahabali and complained that he could never say his prayers in peace. He requested a small parcel of land for his own. All he wanted from Mahabali was land he could measure in three paces.

Shukra, the guru of Mahabali, (5)_____ Vishnu and warned Mahabali that it was probably a trick. Mahabali thought it over, but decided that he would grant the wish of the midget even if it was a trick. As a ruler, he felt (6)_____ to make his subject's lives better.

The midget measured the whole earth in one (7)_____ and the entire Universe in the other. Mahabali offered his head for the third pace and Vishnu pressed him into Pataal, the under-world. Vishnu made Mahabali the ruler of (8)_____.

Table:
danavs, devatas, midget, noble, obligated, pace, Pataal, recognized.

Give yourself 1 star for each correct word that you got.

The correct mappings are (1) danavs (2) devatas (3) noble (4) midget (5) recognized (6) obligated (7) pace (8) Pataal.

Color in the number of stars that you got from the activity on this page.

☆ ☆ ☆ ☆ ☆ ☆ ☆

Vishnu

Three other incarnations of Vishnu are named in the coded messages below. Finish the passage by decoding the words using the table below. Flip the book over to see how many stars you will get from decoding it.

The Earth was over-run by vain and arrogant kings who started to torment

the people. [■ ⊕ ✈ ● ★ ⌘] was born as a human and studied to become

a scholar and a warrior with the name of [⊠ ◇ ⊿ ✈ ● ⌘ ⊿ ◇ □]

who killed the evil kings.

Subsequently, when Hinduism was overrun with meaningless cruel rituals

promoted by ignorant priests, Vishnu was incarnated as [⊕ ⌘ ☆ ☆ ● ◇].

In this form, Vishnu preached against these evil practices. In the future,

another incarnation of Vishnu called [◎ ◇ ⊾ ◎ ⊕] is expected.

Key														
Symbol	◇	⊕	☆	●	⊕	◎	⊾	□	★	⊠	⊿	✈	◆	⌘	■
Letter	A	B	D	H	I	K	L	M	N	P	R	S	T	U	V

Color in the number of stars that you got from the activity on this page.

☆ ☆ ☆ ☆ ☆ ☆ ☆ ☆

Vishnu

All the many names of Vishnu can be very confusing. However, there is one name of Vishnu which is considered equivalent to taking all the thousand names of Vishnu. Figure out that special name by filling in the names of the different pictures shown below. Then rearrange the circled square into the answer.

Flip the book over to see how many stars you will get.

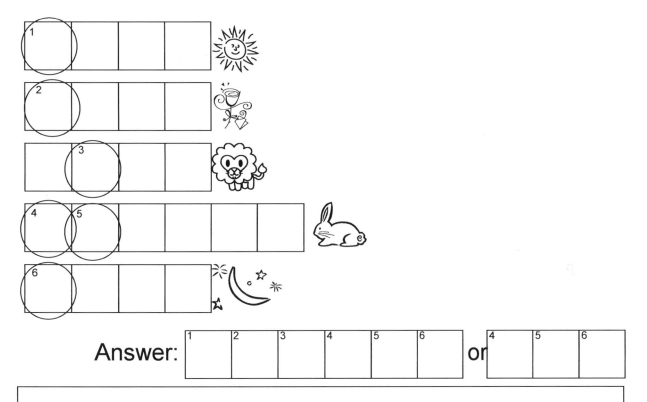

Answer:

The words are SUN, ROSE, LION, RABBIT and MOON. The answer is SRIRAM or RAM.

For each of the words that you got correct, give yourself one star. If you got the answer right as well, give yourself 3 more stars. If you got all the words and the answer right, you will get 8 stars.

Color in the number of stars that you got from the activity on this page.

Ram

Ram is one of the most famous avatars of Vishnu. He was born at the end of treta-yuga. He and his family embody many ideals of Hindi behavior. In the circle shown below, fill in the name of the relative of Ram who is listed on the opposite side of the circle, e.g. enter Sita in the circle opposite Ram's wife.

Flip the book over to see how many stars you will get.

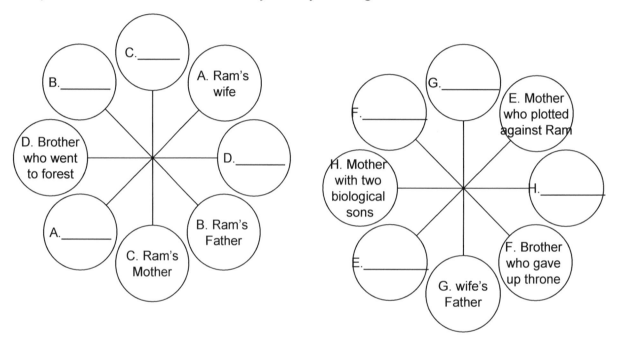

Use names from the following list:
Sita, Dasrath, Kaushalya, Laxman, Kaikayi, Bharat, Janak, Sumitra.

Color in the number of stars that you got from the activity on this page.

Ram

The following story tells the early part of the story of Ram. Fill in the missing words in the right places from the table below.

Dasrath, the king of Ayodha had three wives, but no children. After a lot of attempts, he had four (1)_____ born at an advanced age. The oldest one was Ram, born to his first wife Kaushalya. The second wife Kaikayi had a son called Bharat and the third wife Sumitra had two children, Laxman and Shatrughan. All four of them grew up to be strong and (2)_____.

One day, the sage Viswamitra came to Dasrath and requested the services of Ram and Laxman. His (3)_____ was being attacked by danavas and he wanted warriors to protect himself. When Ram and Laxman were at his hermitage, Viswamitra took them to the Mithila. The King of Mithila, (4)_____ had pledged that his daughter Sita would only be married to a prince who could lift the bow of Shiva he had at his court. Ram easily picked up the (5)_____ and it broke in two. Ram and Sita got married.

Dasrath wanted to give his kingdom to Ram, but Kaikayi forced Dasrath to exile Ram for fourteen years and give the (6)_____ to Bharat instead. Sita and Laxman followed Ram in exile. Dasrath died from the grief of (7)_____ from Ram. Bharat did not like the trickery of his mother and went to get Ram to give the kingdom back to him. The two brothers agreed that Bharat will act as (8)_____ of kingdom till Ram finishes the term of his exile.

Table:
 bow, caretaker, hermitage, Janak, kingdom, separation, sons, valiant,

Color in the number of stars that you got from the activity on this page.

Ram

The story of Ram has many characters. Solve this cross-word puzzle about his life and adventures using the clues provided and the words from the list.

Word List:
Ravan
Hanuman
Kumbhkarn
Vibhishan
Shabri
Sugriv
Bali
Jatayu

Clues:

Down
1. Monkey king killed by Rama
3. Rakshas who befriended Rama
5. Bird that tried to save Sita
7. He kidnapped Sita

Across
2. He slept 6 months and awoke 6 months
4. The monkey king who helped Rama
6. Gave half-eaten fruit to Rama
8. The monkey who found Sita in Lanka

Color in the number of stars that you got from the activity on this page.

Ram

The following paragraphs continue the story of Ram. Fill in the missing words in the right places from the table below.

One day in the forest, Sita saw a beautiful golden deer. She asked Ram to kill the (1)_____ and get its skin. Ram pursued the deer. In a short while, Sita and Laxman heard a shout as if Ram was hurt. Laxman left to check on Ram and Sita was left alone. Ravan, the king of danavs, took the opportunity to kidnap Sita. Jatayu, a (2)_____ whom Ram and Sita had befriended in the forest tried to stop Ravan's air-vehicle, but the old bird was no match for Ravan's sword.

Ram was (3)_____ by the loss of Sita, they started searching for her. The forest dwellers helped them. One of them, Shabri, wanted to make sure Ram only eats sweet fruits and tasted each one before handing them over to Ram. Laxman found that disgusting, but Ram accepted them as a sign of her love.

The two came across a band of (4)_____, who were led by Sugriv. Sugriv was turned out by his (5)_____ Bali, the king of monkeys, who had picked a dispute with him. Ram killed Bali, giving Sugriv the kingdom of Kishkindha, the city of monkeys and (6)_____.

Sugriv dispatched troops of monkeys all over to search for Sita. The group that went South included Hanuman, Angad – the son of Bali and Jamvant – the king of bears. Hanuman found Sita imprisoned in Lanka, the (7)_____ of Ravan. Hearing this, Ram led an (8)_____ of monkeys and bears to Lanka.

Table:
army, bears, brother, deer, devastated, kingdom, monkeys, vulture

Color in the number of stars that you got from the activity on this page.

Ram

The following paragraphs continue the story of Ram. Fill in the missing words in the right places from the table below.

The monkey army arrived at Rameshwaram on the Indian Ocean. With the help of two skilled monkeys, Nal and Neel, Ram built a (1)_____ over the ocean to Lanka and crossed over with his army. He sent Angad as an (2)_____ to Ravan asking him to return Sita. Vibhishan, the brother of Ravan, advised him to return Sita, but Ravan grew (3)_____ and threw Vibhishan out of Lanka. Vibhishan found shelter with Ram.

The war began in earnest. Ranav woke his brother Kumbhkarn, who used to (4)_____ 6 months and was awake only 6 months. Kumbhkarn was a terror, but Ram slew him. Another fierce (5)_____ was Meghnad, the son of Ravan. Laxman killed Meghnad and the tide of war began to turn. After a long and difficult battle, Ram was able to kill Ravan and instated Vibhishan on the throne of (6)_____.

Vibhishan gave Ravan's (7)_____ Pushpak to Ram . Ram, Laxman and Sita returned back to Ayodhya with some of their monkey friends. Bharat was glad to see them and turned the (8)_____ over to Ram. Ram ruled the kingdom in a just and fair way, setting the model for all future rulers. Ram and Sita had twin sons, who were called Luv and Kush.

Table:
 airplane, angry, bridge, envoy, kingdom, Lanka, sleep, warrior,

The correct mappings are (1) bridge (2) envoy (3) angry (4) sleep (5) warrior (6) Lanka (7) aeroplane (8) kingdom.

Give yourself 1 star for each correct word that you got.

Color in the number of stars that you got from the activity on this page.

Ram

In their life and actions, the characters of Ramayan demonstrated the values and actions a person should take. The role models they established is shown on the left side and the action in their life that showed their behavior is shown in the right side. Match the entries in the right and left columns.

Flip the book over to see how many stars you will get.

1. Ideal ruler	A. Ram tried to rescue his wife from strongest king on Earth
2. Ideal husband	B. Ram listened to public opinion even at great personal cost
3. Ideal wife	C. Sita followed her husband in the forest.
4. Ideal brother	D. Laxman accompanied his brother in his exile
5. Ideal son	E. Ran decided to fulfil his father's promises to Kaikayi
6. Ideal father	F. Ram took the exile even though it was most unfair.
7. Ideal warrior	G. Dasrath gave up his life when separated from his son.
8. Ideal subject	H. Ram persisted in battle despite facing fearsome enemies.

Give yourself 1 star for each correct mapping.

The right mapping is 1.B, 2. A, 3. C, 4. D, 5. E, 6. G, 7.H, 8.F. There are many more incidents of similar ideal behavior, e.g. behavior of Bharat as an ideal brother giving up his claims to throne and that of Dasrath as an ideal man fulfilling his word at great personal cost.

Color in the number of stars that you got from the activity on this page.

Krishna

Krishna is one of the most popular incarnations of Vishnu. He was raised by Yashoda on the banks of Yamuna river, but born to different parents in a different place. Solve this cross-word puzzle about his life using the clues provided.

Word List:
Balram
Devaki
Gokul
Kans
Mathura
Nand
Radha
Vasudev

Clues:

Down
1. The brother of Krishna
3. The husband of Yashoda
5. The biological mother of Krishna
7. The place where Krishna was born

Across
2. Girl who loves Krishna with all her heart
4. The biological father of Krishna
6. The evil uncle of Krishna
8. The place where Krishna grows up

Answers: 1. Balram, 2. Radha, 3. Nand, 4. Vasudev, 5. Devaki, 6. Kans, 7. Mathura, 8. Gokul.

Get 1 star for every correct answer.

Color in the number of stars that you got from the activity on this page.

Krishna

The following paragraphs tell the early part of the story of Krishna. Fill in the missing words in the right places from the table below.

Kans, the king of Mathura, heard a prophecy that his death was destined at the hands of his (1)_____. Enraged, he imprisoned his (2)_____ Devaki and her husband Vasudev in the prison for life. If any child was born, he would immediately come and kill it.

A child very dark in complexion was born to Devaki. The guards were asleep and Vasudev stole away with his child. He crossed the raging (3)_____ river to reach his friend Nand in Gokul. Nand had a still-born child earlier and the two friends (4)_____ their children. Then Vasudev returned to his prison.

Krishna grew up in Gokul, standing out with his (5)_____ skin among the group of fair-skinned cowherds around him. He grew up with Balram, the elder son of Devaki. The maidens of Gokul loved Krishna and one girl called Radha was especially fond of him. Cruel Kans suspected that his nephew may still be alive and ordered all young (6)_____ in his kingdom to be killed. However, all evil agents who tried to do this deed in Gokul were foiled by Krishna.

Finally, Kans invited Krishna and Balram to Mathura to his (7)_____. He wanted to kill them there. However, Krishna and Balram destroyed Kans and his evil minions. Krishna (8)_____ his parents and became king of Mathura.

Table:
 children, court, dark, nephew, sister, swapped, Yamuna, freed

Give yourself 1 star for each correct word that you got.

The correct mappings are (1) nephew (2) sister (3) Yamuna (4) swapped (5) dark (6) children (7) court (8) freed.

Color in the number of stars that you got from the activity on this page.

Krishna

Krishna helped a group of princes called the Pandavas through their troubles. The following cross-word puzzle is about the Pandavas and their family. Solve it using the clues provided.

Word List:
Arjun
Bheem
Karn
Kunti
Madri
Nakul
Sahdev
Yudhisthira

Clues:

Down
1. Mother of two youngest Pandavas
3. The eldest Pandav
5. The fourth Pandav
7. The strongest Pandav

Across
2. The best archer among them all
4. A brother of Pandavas, but also an enemy
6. The fifth Pandav
8. The mother of the three elder Pandavas

Color in the number of stars that you got from the activity on this page.

Krishna

The maidens of Gokul missed Krishna. Fill out the missing words in this story to get an important lesson they taught the world. Use the words from the table below.

As the king of Mathura, Krishna found no time to come back to Gokul. The maidens of Gokul (1)_____ him and sent a message to him asking him to return. One of the scholars at the court, Uddhav, thought the maidens were acting (2)_____. He suggested that he preach the path of knowledge to achieve happiness to the maidens and relieve them of their pointless infatuation with Krishna.

Krishna sent Uddhav to Mathura, where he told the maidens to worship the (3)_____ Bramh and follow the path of the knowledge to reach moksha. The maidens listened (4)_____ and then they started to talk about their love for Krishna and how much they loved him with all their heart. They addressed their words to a black wasp that was flying around the garden where they were.

The maidens were so (5)_____ in love with Krishna that Uddhav was overwhelmed by their emotions. Instead of teaching the maidens the path of (6)_____, he realized that the maidens were much closer to God because of their love and (7)_____ to Krishna. He came back a changed person and one who was completely taken over by the path of bhakti.

The poet Surdas has written a sweet set of (8)_____ capturing the maiden's emotions which is known as Bhramar-Geet, or the song of the black wasp.

> Table:
> deeply, devotion, foolish, knowledge, missed, nirguna, patiently, songs.

Give yourself 1 star for each correct word that you got.

The correct mappings are (1) missed (2) foolish (3) nirguna (4) patiently (5) deeply (6) knowledge (7) devotion (8) poems.

Color in the number of stars that you got from the activity on this page.

☆ ☆ ☆ ☆ ☆ ☆ ☆ ☆

Krishna

Krishna also taught the people how to follow the path of action. He did it in the context of the quarrel between the cousins Pandavas and Kauravas. Fill out the missing words from the table in this story to see how he did that.

The Pandavas were (1)_____ sons of King Pandu. Yudhisthira, Arjun and Bheem were sons of his first wife Kunti. Nakul and Sahdev were sons of his (2)_____ wife Madri. Arjun was a very skilled archer, while Bheem was the strongest person in the world. Their cousins were the Kauravas, of whom the oldest was Duryodhan.

Duryodhan (3)_____ the Pandavas and tricked them out of their kingdom and riches by cheating at a game of dice. The Pandavas and their wife Draupadi were (4)_____ badly. After the intervention of the family elders, Duryodhana agreed to return their kingdom if the Pandavs spent thirteen years in exile.

After the (5)_____ period, the Pandavas returned to ask for their lands, but Duryodhan refused to give an inch of land without a fight. The two set of cousins went to (6)_____, supported by different kings of the land. This war is called Mahabharat. On Duryodhan's side were many of the elders and Karn, another son of Kunti whom she had given away at birth.

Before the battle, Arjun lost his will to fight when he saw the family elders on the (7)_____ side. Krishna inspired him to not forsake his duty and to perform his actions as a warrior. This speech, called the Bhagvad Geeta, is considered the (8)_____ guide to following Karma marg or the path of action.

Table:
authoritative, exile, five, hated, insulted, second, war, opposite.

Give yourself 1 star for each correct word that you got.

The correct mappings are (1) five (2) second (3) hated (4) insulted (5) exile (6) war (7) opposite (8) authoritative. And in case you are wondering, the Pandavas won that big war.

Color in the number of stars that you got from the activity on this page.

Shiva

Shiva has many names by which he is called. The table below lists 16 of these names. Find these names in the matrix below. Each name either goes up-down, left-right or diagonally across the matrix using adjacent boxes.

For each word that you get, award yourself with half a star. Round up to the nearest whole star.

Shankar	Mahadev	Mahesh
Tripurari	Bholenath	Natraj
Nagraj	Bhootnath	Chandrasekhar
Trilochan	Rudra	Neelkanth
Shambhu	Har	Asutosh Pasupati

T	R	I	L	O	C	H	A	N	H	I	N	T
R	U	B	H	O	L	E	N	A	T	H	B	R
I	D	H	P	P	A	B	P	T	S	J	B	N
P	R	O	A	P	N	A	G	R	A	J	A	V
U	A	O	S	S	M	A	H	A	D	E	V	H
R	A	T	U	H	A	M	A	J	E	S	H	I
A	S	N	P	I	H	U	M	A	P	A	R	I
R	T	A	A	V	E	A	S	U	T	O	S	H
I	M	T	T	S	S	H	A	N	K	A	R	O
U	B	H	I	S	H	A	M	B	H	U	T	K
C	H	A	N	D	R	A	S	E	K	H	A	R
N	E	E	L	K	A	N	T	H	S	A	P	T

Color in the number of stars that you got from the activity on this page.

Shiva

Shiva has many names and most of these names have a meaning. Match the eight names of Shiva in the left column with the meaning of that name in the right column. Use the hint table below to make your job easy.

1. Mahadev	A. The ruler of all snakes
2. Nagraj	B. The great god
3. Natraj	C. King ruling over all dancers
4. Mahesh	D. One with blue throat
5. Neelkanth	E. The great lord
6. Bhootnath	F. One with moon on the forehead
7. chandrasekhar	G. Enemy of three cities
8. Tripurari	H. master of all ghosts

Hint: Break each name into its sub-words. The you can figure out the meaning using the following meanings of the sub-words.

Maha = great	dev = god	esh = lord
Nag = snakes	raj = king/ruler	nat = dancer
Neel = blue	kanth = throat	Bhoot = ghost
nath = master	chandra = moon	shekhar = head
Tri = three	pur = cities	ari = enemy

The mapping is 1.B, 2. A, 3. C, 4. E, 5. D, 6. H, 7.F, 8.G. Give yourself 1 star for each correct mapping.

Color in the number of stars that you got from the activity on this page.

Shiva

Shiva has many names. One of those names is Tripurari, or the destroyer of three cities. Fill out the missing words from the table in this story to see how Shiva got that name.

When the danavas and devatas were struggling for dominance, a (1)_____ called Mayasur can come up a strategy to control Earth. He created (2)_____ cities in the sky, which would rotate at different speeds in the space. The danav forces stationed themselves in those cities. The cities were well fortified and anyone who attacked one of the three cities would be destroyed by the forces in the other two cities.

With these three cities in the sky, the danavas had total (3)_____ over everyone else. All the devatas came and requested help from Shiva in destroying the three cities. Shiva found out that there was only one way to destroy the three cities. On some occasions in their orbit, the three cities would come together in a (4)_____ and they could be destroyed together by a single missile.

The next time when the three cities were in a straight line, Shiva took his mighty (5)_____ and shot an immense arrow towards the three cities. In one single arrow, the three mighty cities were (6)_____. The devatas were able to take charge of the world once again and to restore order and (7)_____ in the Universe.

For this act, Shiva is called Tripurari. Tri means three, Pur means cities and ari means enemy. Thus, Shiva is the destroyer or (8)_____ of the three cities.

Table:
bow, danav, destroyed, dominance, enemy, line, peace, three.

Give yourself 1 star for each correct word that you got.

The correct mappings are (1) danav (2) three (3) dominance (4) line (5) bow (6) destroyed (7) peace (8) enemy.

Color in the number of stars that you got from the activity on this page.

83

Other Gods

There are many other gods in Hinduism. Solve the following crossword puzzle to figure out the names of some of them. For every god that you are able to get, give yourself one star.

Word List:
Agni
Ganesh
Indra
Kuber
Laxmi
Pavan
Saraswati
Varun

Clues:

Down
1. The god of waters
3. The king of gods
5. The most worthy among gods
7. The goddess of wealth

Across
2. The god of wind
4. The god of fire
6. The goddess of knowledge
8. The treasurer of the gods

Get 1 star for every correct answer.

Answers: 1. Varun, 2. Pavan, 3. Indra, 4. Agni, 5. Ganesh, 6. Saraswati, 7. Laxmi, 8. Kuber.

Color in the number of stars that you got from the activity on this page.

Other Gods

Now that you have learnt about so many different gods and goddesses of Hinduism, Match the pictures of some of the gods with their names.

Flip the book over to see how many stars you will get.

1. Durga

A

2. Laxmi

B

3. Ganesh

C

4. Ram

D

The right mapping is 1.A, 2. C, 3. D, 4. B.

Give yourself 2 stars for each correct mapping.

Color in the number of stars that you got from the activity on this page.

Ganesh

In any worship or rituals, Ganesh is the god who is worshipped first. He is considered the most worthy among all the gods. The following narrative explains how Ganesh came to get this honor. Fill out the missing words from the table in this story to complete the story.

At the beginning of the time, the (1)_____ were happy to hear that they would be worshipped by the humans. But they all started fighting among themselves as to who ought to be (2)_____ first. Each of them thought he or she should be the person who was worshipped first.

They appealed to Shiva to settle the dispute and he suggested a small (3)_____ among them. They would all need to go around the world twenty-one times stopping at the different places of pilgrimage and the god who (4)_____ first to Shiva would be the most worthy and be worshipped first.

All the gods jumped on their (5)_____ and rushed off to finish the challenge, all except Ganesha. He realized that his mount, the puny (6)_____, was no match for the swifter mounts of the others. He thought he would just go around his parents, Shiva and Parvati, twenty-one times while he waited for the others to finish the race and return.

Each of the other gods saw that Ganesh was just (7)_____ any site they had just arrived to. All of them conceded the competition to Ganesh. Ganesh was not sure what happened until Shiva explained – devotion to one's (8)_____ makes one more worthy than visiting all the places of pilgrimage.

Table:
competition, gods, leaving, mounts, mouse, parents, returned, worshipped.

Color in the number of stars that you got from the activity on this page.

☆☆☆☆☆☆☆☆

Hindu Festivals

Introduction

Like all great religions, a big part of Hinduism is its festivals. There are many festivals that are celebrated by Hindus. Because Hinduism allows a complete freedom in the choice of the form of Bramh that one chooses to worship, the number of festivals is huge. Different festivals are celebrated in different regions.

Many of the festivals celebrate the events and people associated with the legends you studied in the previous section. Some of them are devoted to specific gods, i.e. specific manifestations of the Saakaar Bramh.

In this section, there is a brief introduction to some of the major festivals celebrated by Hindus all over the world.

Hindu Festivals

There are many Hindu festivals, some of which are listed in the tabe below. Find these names in the matrix below. Each name either goes up-down, left-right or diagonally across the matrix using adjacent boxes.

For each word that you get, award yourself with half a star. Round up to the nearest whole star.

Rakhi	Navratri	Ramnavami
Mahashivratri	MakarSankranti	Vijaydashmi
Bhaidooj	Janmashtami	KarwaChauth
Mahakumbh	Pongal	Onam
Teej	Holi	Diwali Vaishakhi

M	K	S	P	M	B	H	A	I	D	O	O	J	S
P	A	N	I	A	T	H	V	I	I	D	A	A	M
S	R	S	N	H	L	A	A	H	W	S	S	N	A
T	W	I	P	R	D	A	M	K	A	J	I	M	H
M	A	A	O	N	A	M	K	D	L	A	A	A	A
V	C	K	N	A	R	A	K	H	I	M	A	S	S
A	H	A	G	V	H	H	T	E	E	J	K	H	H
M	A	K	A	R	S	A	N	K	R	A	N	T	I
E	U	M	L	A	M	K	A	B	D	R	A	A	V
H	T	N	I	T	I	U	A	A	I	A	N	M	R
I	H	M	H	R	A	M	N	A	V	A	M	I	A
L	O	M	A	I	A	B	M	I	X	U	P	K	T
S	L	V	A	I	S	H	A	K	H	I	J	O	R
T	I	A	V	I	J	A	Y	D	A	S	H	M	I

Color in the number of stars that you got from the activity on this page.

Hindu Festivals

One of the big festivals for Hindus is the festival of Diwali. Fill out the missing words from the table in this story to see the festival got started.

At the end of the Treta-yuga in the current chaturyuga cycle, prince Ram of the (1)_____ of Kosal had to leave the (2)_____ Ayodhya and live in the forest for fourteen years. His wife Sita and brother Laxman went along with him.

In the forest, a evil danav called Ravan (3)_____ Sita. Ravan was the strongest ruler among all species of living beings at that time. Ram made friends with a group of (4)_____ and bears and with their help defeated Ravan. He freed Sita and the trio of Ram, Sita and Laxman returned to Ayodhya.

The (5)_____ of Ayodhya were happy to see Ram back. They celebrated his arrival by lighting (6)_____ and distributing sweets. Since then, the tradition started to celebrate the return of the prince every year.

Diwali is celebrated on the night of the new (7)_____ in the month of Kartik. There are other (8)_____ associated with the festival, one of them being that Laxmi, the goddess of wealth, visits the earth on that day and looks out for lighted houses. The festival is celebrated with lights, firecrackers and sweets and is a fun event for all.

Table:
capital, kidnapped, kingdom, lamps, legends, moon, monkeys, people.

Give yourself 1 star for each correct word that you got.

The correct mappings are (1) kingdom (2) capital (3) kidnapped (4) monkeys (5) people (6) lamps (7) moon (8) legends.

Color in the number of stars that you got from the activity on this page.

☆ ☆ ☆ ☆ ☆ ☆ ☆

Hindu Festivals

Many Hindu festivals celebrate the birth of a great hero from the legends. They are birthday parties except the birthday is computed according to the traditional Hindu calendar. Decode some of these birthday parties using the code below.

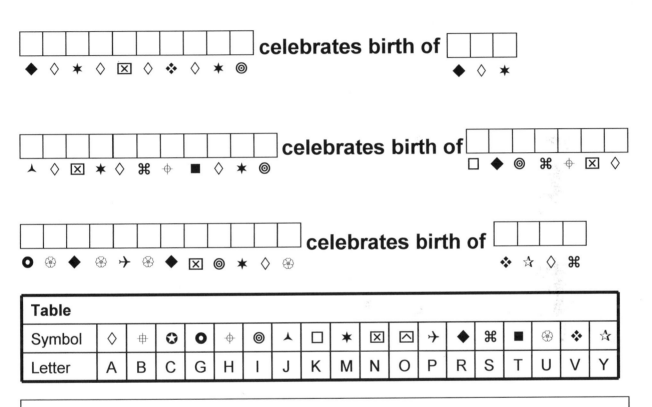

Table																		
Symbol	◇	⊕	✪	●	⊕	◎	⋏	□	★	⊠	⊡	✈	◆	⌘	■	❀	❖	☆
Letter	A	B	C	G	H	I	J	K	M	N	O	P	R	S	T	U	V	Y

Ramanavami celebrates birth of Ram, Janmashtami celebrates birth of Krishna and Guru Purnima celebrates birth of Vyas. Vyas is an Indian sage who wrote many of the important scriptures including the four vedas and the eighteen purans. Many other Indian festivals also are birthday celebrations including the festivals of Ganesh Chaturthi (birth of Ganesh) and Hanuman Jayanti (birth of Hanuman).

Give yourself 8 stars if you get all six words right, otherwise 1 star for each word you get right.

Color in the number of stars that you got from the activity on this page.

91

Hindu Festivals

Another important festival is that of Holi. Fill out the missing words from the table in this story to see the festival got started.

Prahlad was the son of the king of danavs, but he was a great (1)_____ of Vishnu. This enraged his father tremendously and he (2)_____ to get his son killed. The king had a sister called Holika who had a magic blanket. This blanket would protect anyone wearing it from fire.

The evil pair of brother and sister (3)_____ a plan. Aunt Holika will sit in a roaring bonfire with Prahlad in her lap. Her (4)_____ blanket will protect her, while the naughty prince who dared to like Vishnu would be burnt. They executed on that plan.

However, Vishnu caused a (5)_____ to blow as soon as Holika stepped into the fire. The wind blew the blanket around Prahlad (6)_____ him and exposing the evil aunt. She was burnt to a crisp. The people were overjoyed at the news that Prahlad survived. They celebrated by throwing colors on each other.

At present time, people have a big (7)_____ called Holika the night before Holi. The next day, people throw colored powder and water on each other. Holi falls on the last new moon day in the month of Phalgun. The festival is celebrated in many different parts of India and is known by other (8)_____ such as Dhulendi, Dolyatra, Phag and Basan-utsav.

Table:
 bonfire, decided, devotee, hatched, magic, names, protecting, wind.

Color in the number of stars that you got from the activity on this page.

☆ ☆ ☆ ☆ ☆ ☆ ☆

Hindu Festivals

Many Hindu festivals celebrate the relations that exist in the family and the society. Match some of the relationships to the festivals they celebrate. Put in the name of the festival against the ball showing the relationship.

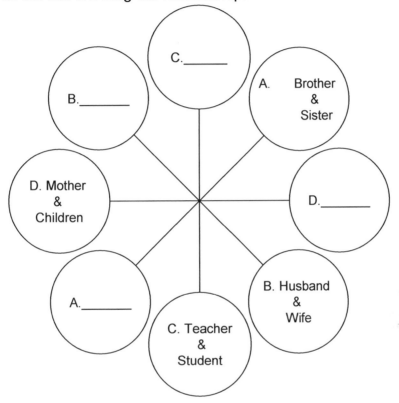

Use festivals from the following list: **Rakhi, Karwa Chauth, Teej, Guru Purnima.**

The answers are A. Rakhi, B. Karwa Chauth, C. Guru Purnima, D. Teej. For each of the words that you got correct, give yourself two stars.

Color in the number of stars that you got from the activity on this page.

93

Hindu Festivals

Several festivals in India are marked to celebrate the return of a hero or heroine to their native land. Fill in the missing words in the passage below to know of some of these festivals in India.

Mahabali was a great (1)_____ king who was very pious and devout. He was tricked out of his kingdom by (2)_____ in the incarnation of a midget. However, Vishnu was so impressed with Mahabali that he made him the king of Pataal, the world that exists underneath the Earth.

Mahabali loved his (3)_____ who lived on Earth and his subjects adored their noble king. Therefore, he requested permission from Vishnu that he be allowed to visit to his subjects once every year. The festival of Onam is celebrated in the state of Kerala to mark the annual (4)_____ of Mahabali.

During Onam, people make (5)_____ decorations outside their homes to welcome back Mahabali. There is feasting, singing, (6)_____ and merriment. This is also the occasion of the famous boat race of Kerala.

In the region of Bihar, another return is celebrated during the festival of Chath. Chath celebrates the (7)_____ return of Chathi Maiya, considered the daughter and presiding (8)_____ of Bihar. People worship the setting sun and the rising sun on the sixth day after Diwali to ask for the blessings of the Chatthi Maiya.

Table:
annual, danav, dancing, deity, floral, return, subjects, Vishnu.

Give yourself 1 star for each correct word that you got.

(8) deity.

The correct mappings are (1) danav (2) Vishnu (3) subjects (4) return (5) floral (6) dancing (7) annual

Color in the number of stars that you got from the activity on this page.

☆ ☆ ☆ ☆ ☆ ☆ ☆

Hindu Festivals

There are many more festivals in Hinduism in different regions of India than can be covered properly in this book. Listed below are some of the festivals and some of the actions that people do in the celebration of those festivals. Match the festival against the thing that people do.

1. Holi	A. People in Gujarat dance with sticks
2. Diwali	B. People throw colors at each other
3. Onam	C. People cook rice and let it overflow
4. Pongal	D. People burn a statue of Ravan
5. Dussehara	E. There is a famous boat race in Kerala
6. Navaratri	F. People eat a sweet called modak.
7. Rakhi	G. People burst firecrackers and light lamps
8. Ganesh Chaturthi	H. Sisters tie a thread on their brother's wrist

The mapping is 1.B, 2. G, 3. E, 4. C, 5. D, 6. A, 7.H, 8.F. Give yourself 1 star for each correct mapping.

Navatri is celebrated in Gujarat with a dance called Garba which uses sticks. In Pongal, one of the rituals is to boil the new harvest of rice till it boils over. It is celebrated in Tamil Nadu. Onam in Kerala has very exciting boat races. In Dussehara, also called Vijaydashmi, people celebrate the death of Ravan at the hands of Ram by burning his effigy. And on Ganesh Chaturthi, celebrated vigorously in Maharastra, modak is the preferred sweet.

Color in the number of stars that you got from the activity on this page.

Hindu Festivals

Some festivals in India have more than one legend about their origins. Fill in the missing words in the passage below to know of a legend about the festival of Rakhi.

The great king of danavs, Mahabali ruled Pataal, the underworld. He was given that kingdom by Vishnu. Mahabali had requested that (1)_____ come and protect his kingdom from the various enemies. Vishnu could not deny that request. Mahabali was (2)_____ and pious and he had many enemies specially among the devatas.

Vishnu had to spend his entire time (3)_____ the kingdom of Mahabali. This made his wife Laxmi very sad. She wanted Vishnu to come back and look after the entire world. In order to do so, she took the form of a poor woman and went asking for help from Mahabali. On the day of the full moon in the month of Sravan, (4)_____ tied a thread on the wrist of Mahabali.

Mahabali asked the poor woman to ask for any (5)_____. He said that the women should consider him like a (6)_____. The poor woman said that she just wanted her husband back home. Mahabali promised that he will find her husband and get him back. Laxmi revealed her true form and pleaded that Mahabali release Vishnu from his pledge to protect Pataal day and night.

Mahabali (7)_____ and he let Vishnu return back to his home. Since that day, sisters tie a (8)_____ on the wrist of their brothers on that day to celebrate the occasion. The brothers promise to protect their sisters on this occasion.

> Table:
> agreed, brother, gift, guarding, just, thread, Laxmi, Vishnu.

Give yourself 1 star for each correct word that you got.

The correct mappings are (1) Vishnu (2) just (3) guarding (4) Laxmi (5) gift (6) brother (7) agreed (8) thread.

Color in the number of stars that you got from the activity on this page.

Hindu Calendar

Hindu Time-Keeping

The Hindu scholars have a very sophisticated scale for counting time. It goes from sub-seconds to eons. Let us look at the time-keeping units used for a day or less.

The units of time-keeping in Hindu mythology is nimesh, kastha, kalaa and muhurt. They have the following relationship.

> 15 nimesh = 1 kastha
> 30 kastha = 1 kalaa
> 30 kalaas = 1 muhurt
> 30 muhurt = 1 day (i.e. a 24 hour period)

Another common division is a prahar. A 24 hour period of day and night is divided into 8 prahars of equal duration.

Fill in the missing numbers in the questions below, rounding all answers to nearest integers. Flip the book to see how many stars you get based on your answers.

A. 1 second equals _____ nimesh.

B. 1 muhurt equals _____ minutes.

C. 1 prahar equals _____ hours

D. If a good muhurt started at 1 PM, it will finish at _____ PM.

You may have heard of people taking about a good muhurt for doing something like a wedding. Now you know what it means. In traditional Indian astrology, some people believe that some times are better for doing some type of actions. The period during which the good times will last is usually a muhurt.

A is 5 seconds (4.6875 to be exact). B is 48. C is 3 and D. is 1:48 PM. Give yourself two stars for each correct answer.

Color in the number of stars that you got from the activity on this page.

Hindu Time-Keeping

The next scale of time-keeping is in months and years. The divisions of time for that period in Hindu tradition are as follows:

15 days = 1 paksha
2 paksha = 1 maas
6 maas = 1 ayan
2 ayan = 1 year

The ayan in which the Sun in North of the equator is called Uttarayan (Uttar = North) and the ayan in which the Sun is South of the equator is called Dakshinayan (Dakshin = South).

The 15 days of a paksha correspond to the waxing and waning of the moon. The krishna (black) paksha is when moon's ligthed area is decreasing (i.e. from full moon to new moon) and the shukla (white) paksha is when moon's visible area increases, i.e. from new moon to full moon.

Fill in the missing words in the questions below. Flip the book to see how many stars you get based on your answers.

A. 1 ayan equals _____ months.

B. 1 maas equals about _____ days.

C. In the shukla paksh, the moon _____ in size.

D. The fact that months are counted by the phases of the moon means the Hindu calendar is a _____ one. (pick from lunar or solar)

A is 6, B is 30. C is increases and D is lunar. Give yourself two stars for each correct answer.

Color in the number of stars that you got from the activity on this page.

Hindu Months

The traditional Hindu year is divided into twelve months that follow the cycles of the moon. A month consists of a shukla paksha and a krishna paksha. The twelve months name in Sanskrit are as follows. Chaitra is the first month and begins in the February-March period.

1. Chaitra
2. Vaishākh
3. Jyaishtha
4. Ashadha
5. Shravana
6. Bhadrapad
7. Ashwin
8. Kartik
9. Margashirsha
10. Paush
11. Magh
12. Phalgun

The twelve lunar months don't match precisely with the solar cycle of 365 days, so an additional month is added every 2-3 years. Hindu traditional calendar years are expressed in either the Shaka Samvat, in which year 0 begins in 78 A.D., or the Vikram Samvat in which year 0 begins in 56 B.C.

Some of these names have common colloquial versions of the names. Match the colloquial names to the proper names by looking at the similarities.

A. Jeth
D. Bhadon
B. Chait
E. Poos
C. Sawan
F. Phagua

A-3(Jyestha), B-1(chaitra), C-5(Shravana), D-6(Bhadrapad), E-10(Paush), F-12(Phalgun). Give yourself one star for each correct answer and 2 bonus stars if you get all 6 right.

Color in the number of stars that you got from the activity on this page.

Four Yugas

A key concept in Hindu time-keeping is the concept of yugas. There are four yugas. To get the nams of the four yugas, cross out all the C, M, Z and Xs from the figure below. Then copy the remaining letters down below to see the name of the four yugas

CSZAXCTAKYCZUXGCZAM

MDZWXACAXPCACXRCZAC

TCZRXETAMYCZUXGCZAX

CKZAXCLIMYCZUXGCZAM

Color in the number of stars that you got from the activity on this page.

Four Yugas

The yugas occur in a cycle of time which is known together as a chaturyuga (four yugas). The total time for a chaturyuga is 17,28,000 years for Satayuga, 1,296,000 years for Treta, 864,000 years for Dwapar and 432,000 years for Kaliyuga.

1000 cycles of the chaturguya make a Kalp. A kalp is also known as a single day of Bramha.

According to legends, the entire Universe is created at the beginning of the day of Bramha. The Universe is destroyed at the end of the day and there is nothing but void for the night of Bramha, which is same in duration as the day of Bramha. Then the next day of Bramha, the Universe is created once again.

The life-time of Bramha is 100 Bramha-years, i.e. 36,000 Kalps, after which the current Bramha (and other gods) die and a new one born to continue the cycle again.

In each day of Bramha, there are 14 Manavantaras of equal duration. In each Manavanatara, a new Manu (the progenitor of humans) and other attending stars in the sky is in existence.

The current time according to Hindu calendar since the start of the current Bramha is

51 Bramha Years,
1st Bramha Day (Kalpa)
Seventh Manvantara
28th Chaturyuga
about 5000 years since start of Kaliyuga

Tallying Up the stars

Keep track of the stars you have obtained on different pages and then sum them up at the bottom of the page. Write down the stars you get on each page, then sum up the columns and then add the sums in the columns to get the grand total.

Page	Stars	Page	Stars	Page	Stars	Page	Stars	Page	Stars
7		26		46		67		86	
8		27		47		68		89	
9		28		48		69		90	
10		29		49		70		91	
11		30		50		71		92	
12		31		53		72		93	
13		32		54		73		94	
14		33		55		74		95	
15		34		56		75		96	
16		35		57		76		98	
17		36		58		77		99	
18		37		59		78		100	
19		38		60		79		101	
20		39		61		80			
21		40		62		81			
22		42		63		82			
23		43		64		83			
24		44		65		84			
25		45		66		85			
Total		Total		Total		Total		Total	
Grand Total									

Tallying Up the stars

Count the total number of stars you have collected in this entire book.
You can now qualify your knowledge of Hinduism in the following categories.

Number of Stars	Your level	Meaning of level
0-49	Agyani	Ignorant
50-99	Alpagya	With some knowledge
100-199	Gyani	Knowledgeable
200-299	Mahagyani	Very knowledgeable
300-399	Rishi	Scholar
400-499	Maharishi	Great Scholar
500-599	Rajarshi	Royal Scholar
600 or more	Bramharishi	Ultimate Scholar

Publications of Chanda Books

Level 1 Hindi:
Aamoo the Aam
Aamoo the Aam – Part II
Aamoo the Aam – Part III
Hindi Children's Book Level 1 Easy Reader

Level 2 Hindi:
Tara Sitara
Tara ke Kisse
Hindi Children's Book Level 2 Easy Reader

Level 3 Hindi:
Sonu ke Kisse
Sonu ke Afsane
Sonu ke Tyohar
Hindi Children's Book Level 3 Easy Reader

Activity Books:
Learn Hindi Alphabet Activity Workbook
Learn Hindi Vocabulary Activity Workbook
Learn Hindi Grammar Activity Workbook
Hindi Activity Workbook
Hinduism for Children Activity Workbook
Learn Bengali Alphabet Activity Workbook
Learn Bengali Vocabulary Activity Workbook

Alphabet Books:
Bengali Alphabet Book
Gujarati Alphabet Book
Hindi Alphabet Book
Marathi Alphabet Book
Punjabi Alphabet Book

Others:
Bhajan Ganga
Indian Culture Stories: Sanskar
South Asian Immigration Stories

For an updated list, visit us at http://www.chandabooks.com

Made in the USA
San Bernardino, CA
23 February 2016